Style IN PROSE FICTION

Style IN PROSE FICTION

ENGLISH INSTITUTE ESSAYS · 1958

Edited with a Foreword by Harold C. Martin

Columbia University Press

NEW YORK AND LONDON

Foreword

In the Dedicatory Letter to *Man and Superman,* George Bernard Shaw observes that, though style is impossible without statement, it is style, not statement, that persists: "Disprove [an] assertion after it is made, yet its style remains." And, of course, only that assertion which goes beneath the surface, behind the moment, has any chance of escaping later emendation or disproof. "It is not the purpose of literature to purvey news. For news consult the *Almanac de Gotha,*" Melville warns the reader on behalf of his principals Jack Gentian and the Marquis de Grandvin. Since literature is, above all, matter which persists, not news though always new, it would seem that the literary critic must then take as his first concern that property of literature most characteristic of its persistence and of its enduring novelty. When he thinks of literature, the literary critic must think first of style.

The same need not be said of the scholar, whose proper concerns may be more extensive. Yet literary critic and scholar must, in the end, agree. Whether he begins from textual variants, formal tradition, the history of an idea, or the elaboration of a literary movement, the scholar must lay his tribute at the foot of the original document, the poem. Just so, studies in prosody and idiomatology and tropism must all yield what they mine to a unity of a different order and kind than their own. That unity is the literary work, and its *anima* is style.

It is principally around this doctrine of the paramount importance of style that our modern battle of the books has been waged. In the United States, the shibboleth of the protagonist has been the "new criticism," a watchword which the Gileadites of literary historical persuasion have found sufficient for distinguishing all manner of heretics from the faithful. Thus the epithet "new critic" has become generic for all students of literature who assert the autonomy of the literary work, regardless whether they approach it with archetypal, pyschoanalytic, linguistic, ideological, or rhetorical preoccupations. The fact that the "new criticism" now means so much that it means nothing much at all is one sign that it has carried the day; it is also a sign that, in winning, it has compromised a great deal of what it set out to keep pure.

The earliest "new criticism" in the United States was mainly, and often exclusively, concerned with rhetoric, with the expressive characteristics of a given literary piece. It developed from the tradition of *explications de texte* which was introduced in France at the end of the nineteenth century in reaction to the excessive literary historicism of the time. Behind that critical and pedagogical practice, supporting it and then going well beyond it, there is a strong tradition of Swiss, German, and Dutch scholarship in the elements of style and in their significance. *Stilforschung*—the name that tradition still bears despite a marked change in premises over the past eighty years—was, at first, part of the passionate positivist effort of

the nineteenth century to catalogue and explain all the phenomena of human existence. Its methods were formidably
empirical to the point of generalization and, at that point, even
more formidably imaginative. What Alexander von Humboldt
did not hesitate to attempt for the cosmos other scholars had
no reason to hesitate about attempting for the works of a single
author, a literary generation, a nation, or even an epoch.

Inevitably such ambitious undertakings drew the *Stilforscher*
away from the purely linguistic elements of his subject matter
well into the realms of psychology, anthropology, and sociology.
And, quite as inevitably, they led him to see the individual
literary work more and more in terms of a matrix, and to
describe it as the expression not so much of individual insight
and skill as of forces for which the artist was little more than a
vehicle. The theoretical one-sidedness of this view and its
damaging effect on the status of literature had two immediate
results: a revolt against all systematizing of literary observation
and concomitant insistence on the primacy of subjective response;
and Benedetto Croce's esthetic doctrine of the integrity of the
literary work as an artifact, a doctrine which predicated the
obligation of the literary critic to understand that work as the
expression of experience isolated in and tempered by the psyche
of its creator.

Because the first of these reactions to historicism offered no
attraction for their discipline, philologists in the *Stilforschung*
tradition have tended to follow the lead of the second. The
result has been studies which may be classified roughly, in two
groups. "Formalist" studies (those of Roman Jakobson are
probably best known in this country) use the refinements of

linguistic learning to relate the phonemic, syntactical, and semantic aspects of a work. There is no satisfactory name for the other group though "psychoanalytic" suggests itself since the concern is to find, through analysis of stylistic properties, the harmony of conception and execution in a work, and since that harmony is construed as the reflection of a psychic harmony in the writer. Professor Leo Spitzer, a leading practitioner who has used the term *Werkstudien* to describe some of his own investigation, makes the position clear in his study of the style of Charles Péguy: "Man muss sich nur in die *Seele des Schriftstellers* versenken (was natürlich beim Herausreissen eines Stückes aus dem rein lokalen und vor allem dem seelischen Zusammenhang nicht möglich ist), um das Warum dieses Stiles zu verstehen" (*Stilstudien,* II, 304).

The possibility of such studies depends, of course, in no small measure on the careful research in language which is a principal contribution of scholarship to the twentieth century. Of general relevance to stylistics was the work of such grammarians as Jespersen and Curme; of more immediate relevance such painstaking studies as that of the relationship between literary and "ordinary" language begun by Charles Bally, or the analysis of the meaningfulness of syntax which is associated particularly with the name of Eugen Lerch. To name so few in the list of important figures would be invidious were not Helmut Hatzfeld's *Critical Bibliography of the New Stylistics* (Chapel Hill, N. C., 1953) readily available. The one observation that may be pertinent about the others is that, theorists and practitioners alike, they are predominantly European, even though some of the most distinguished—Professors Spitzer and Jakobson, already mentioned, and the late Amado Alonso, for example—hold, or held, chairs in American universities.

Where stylistic criticism has affected the study of literature in the United States, poetry has been the principal beneficiary— partly because relative brevity is an asset for the scholar studying all aspects of the language in a literary work and partly, no doubt, because the strong interest in euphony and rhythm of stylistic "formalists" naturally leads them toward literary forms in which those elements are most important to meaning. There is, to be sure, no dearth of books in English on "style," many of them instructive, a few deeply thoughtful, but almost none really systematic or, indeed, clearly committed to the concept of style as the fundamental structural component of a literary work. And the past twenty years have produced a flood of "explica- tions," though these again have less often demonstrated system than ingenuity, less often a carefully disciplined understanding of language than a facility at reconciling the possibilities of irony, paradox, and ambiguity as though obliquity and devious- ness were the only *lingua franca* of the artist. Good stylistic criticism, though sparse, has not been entirely lacking, as the bibliography at the end of this volume will suggest; but sig- nificant contributions by American scholars either to theoretical stylistics or to the application of stylistic procedures in literary criticism have been few.

The seven essays that make up this volume do not by any means presume to correct our laggardness in this field of scholarship. They represent, indeed, no more than efforts to investigate some of the possibilities inherent in the method of intrinsic analysis as it may be applied to prose texts. Three of the papers were first read at the English Institute in 1957 in the conference on prose style in American fiction; the four which compose the first half of the volume come from an extension of that conference, in 1958, into English fiction. All but one of the essays may, without great violence to the term, be called "practical criticism." Two of them—the one by Dr. Strauss and my own—limit themselves to vocabulary and syntax, Dr. Strauss's in a paragraph by Smollett, mine in paragraphs by Cooper and Crane. The first explains the stylistic peculiarities of its paragraph by reference to other parts of Smollett's work; the second uses its two paragraphs as a starting point for the discussion of some changes in narrative sensibility over the course of a century. Professor Gerber's essay argues that Mark Twain's style is not only inseparable but derivative from his point of view; Professor Craig's that verbal perplexities in Thackeray's *Vanity Fair* dissolve when a scrupulously designed passage of description is read metaphorically as the key to a style that not only contains but obviously exploits those perplexities. In Professor Johnson's essay the effect of a conscious "borrowing" on Hardy's style is carefully documented; in Professor Crow's the effect of James's much more conscious effort to avoid borrowings, even from the linguistic conventions of the time, is the subject of persuasive analysis. The remaining essay, printed first in the volume, is Mr. Ohmann's argument on "modernist" philosophical grounds for the reasonableness of the study of style as a primary literary concern. It may profitably be read in conjunction with an earlier English Institute paper by Professor Craig La Drière, which makes a similar case on entirely different grounds (*English Institute Essays, 1948*).

Neither in the organization of the two conferences nor in the preparation of this volume was there any clear intention to provide a spectrum of approaches to the study of style. The diversity of the essays that follow, like their congruity, is undesigned except as all start from the concept of style as a writer's conscious or subconscious choice among alternatives offered by a language for the expression of thought or feeling.

HAROLD C. MARTIN

Cambridge, Massachusetts
January, 1959

Contents

Richard M. Ohmann

Prolegomena to the Analysis
of Prose Style

The considerations of this essay are of a very primitive sort. If they are prolegomena to the study of style, they are preliminary by several stages to the study of style in the novel. What is more, a few decades ago they would have seemed utterly superfluous to most rhetoricians, who were quite content to think of style as the verbal dress of disembodied thought. Yet now comes a school of criticism which aims to discredit the split between form and content, a school which argues that no two different utterances mean the same thing, and, more radically that, "every statement is a unique style of its own."[1] This organicist position, in spite of its stringency, has appealed increasingly to critic and linguist alike.[2] In fact it has nearly attained the status of dogma, of an official motto, voiced in the triumphant tones of reason annihilating error. Appealing as the

[1] Andrews Wanning, "Some Changes in the Prose Style of the Seventeenth Century" (Ph.D. dissertation, University of Cambridge, 1938), p. 20.

[2] An example of the linguist's position: "It is a well-tried hypothesis of linguistics that formally different utterances always differ in meaning. . . ." Leonard Bloomfield, "Linguistic Aspects of Science," *International Encyclopedia of Unified Science*, I (Chicago, 1955), 253.

idea is, commonplace though it has lately become in criticism, semantics, and linguistics, it would seem to render futile most extant stylistic analysis, if not to undercut the whole idea of style. For if style does not have to do with *ways* of saying *something,*[3] just as style in tennis has to do with ways of hitting a ball, is there anything at all which is worth naming "style"? If not, most critics of style have really given us judgments about what writers mean, masquerading as judgments about manner. The critic can talk about what the writer says, but talk about style he cannot, for his neat identity—one thought, one form— allows no margin for individual variation, which is what we ordinarily mean by style. Style, then, becomes a useless hypothetical construct half way between meaning and the person who means, and the study of style would seem to be the moribund offspring of a prolific reification: the assumption that because there is a word "style," there must be a thing to match.

Confronted with this dilemma, the conscientious critic can only say, with Wittgenstein, "Whereof one cannot speak, thereof one must be silent," and rejoice at the elimination of another pseudo-discipline. The trouble with this ascetic solution is that the critic may still feel it useful to speak of style. If he *is* unwilling to see stylistics tossed into the positivist's scrap-heap,

[3] Here, as with too many pseudo-philosophical problems, ordinary language seems to have been the villain. Our speech makes a separation between saying and thing said: one *says it*. And if expressing is an action that one performs on an idea, just as hitting is an action performed on a tennis ball, why not different *ways* of expressing an idea? The distinction works with vocal speech, for the same words can be spoken with different stress, pitch, tone, and so forth; but a moment's reflection shows that it does not apply to the written word, and that any approach to stylistics empowered by a split between form and content is in serious theoretical trouble.

along with ethics and metaphysics, he may work out a compromise: the most common is to say that style is part of what
we ordinarily call meaning,[4] that it is peripheral meaning, or
subterranean meaning, or connotative meaning. Such a solution
is fruitful, I think, but it leads to a new problem. If style
exists, by courtesy of this redefinition, where are its boundaries?
Which part of meaning is to be called style, and which is really
meaning? In short, how can we tell style from not-style?

These difficulties are not, I hope, mere compliant straw men
to be handily blown down. They are real, and they are crucial,
for on their resolution depend answers to these questions: What
is style? What kind of scrutiny will it reward? What can it
show about the writer?

I

Let me begin the argument, unabashedly, where so many
critical arguments begin—with I. A. Richards.

Socrates is wise.

Wisdom belongs to Socrates.

Mr. Richards offers these two sentences as a capsule demonstration of the way in which we "can put one thought form
into many different word patterns."[5] He does not, as he may
seem to do, neatly sever form and content; he is arguing a more
subtle case, and one which ends by leaving form and content
neither quite joined nor totally separated—a happy compromise,
seemingly, for the beleaguered would-be critic of style. Let us
examine it.

---

[4] This is Mr. Wanning's theoretical justification for proceeding with his study.
[5] *Interpretation in Teaching* (New York, 1938), p. 285.

Mr. Richards uses the example concerning the wisdom of Socrates in a discussion calculated to refute J. S. Mill's contention that "the principles and rules of grammar are the means by which the forms of language are made to correspond with the universal forms of thought."[6] On the contrary, argues Mr. Richards, anyone who wishes to predicate wisdom of Socrates may cast his thought in one of several molds. Conversely, in English, thoughts of incompatible forms often take the same syntactical shape: for example, "I see a tiger" and "I kick a tiger." It is obvious that to kick a tiger is to act on it, whereas to see a tiger is to be affected in a complicated way by it. Mr. Richards submits that the tiger would no doubt administer a terminal lesson in logic to the man who confused sentence forms with forms of thought in this disastrous fashion.

His contention that the two sentences about Socrates express *congruent* thoughts is not, however, a contention that they express the *same idea,* or mean the *same thing,* or are *equivalent.* In one statement Socrates is the given quantity; in the other, wisdom. One sentence works by limiting the denotation of "Socrates," by eliminating possible statements such as "Socrates is stupid," and "Socrates is foolish." The other sentence focuses on a set of attributes and ways of behaving called "wisdom," and tells of one point in space-time where we can find it, namely in Socrates. One sentence belongs in a context of curiosity about Socrates; it might come in answer to the question, "What sort of mind had Socrates?" The other might satisfy someone who is looking, not for an honest, but for a wise man. The two sentences differ in the type of information given, in

[6] *Inaugural Lecture at St. Andrews,* quoted by Richards, p. 280.

pattern of emphasis, in the sort of expectation they satisfy. In short, they say different things.

Rather than artificially separating idea from expression, Mr. Richards suggests that ideas fall into a finite set of categories, according to logical shape or form. His medial position between a dualism of manner and matter which is currently heretical, and a monism which is orthodox but fatal, allows to style a tenuous existence as the manner of clothing ethereal forms of thought in neatly tailored word patterns.[7] Under the aegis of this theory the study of a writer's style becomes the examination of the formal changes he works on each group of ideas, of the metamorphoses through which he puts each form of thought.

Attractive as this theory may seem to the critic who wishes to talk about style, but is hard put to see what style is, I think it must be rejected, even at the cost, possibly, of a final lesson in logic from Mr. Richards's tiger. For one thing, these shadowy forms of thought are so indistinguishable from each other, so nearly hidden by overlapping word patterns, that, rather than implementing a rigorous criticism, they would make it inhumanly difficult. Mr. Richards's distinction between seeing and kicking a tiger is easy enough to follow; one idea is of the form "*a* receives sense data from *b*," and the other is of the form "*a* acts on *b*." But what of the sentence "I feel a tiger"? To which form of thought does it belong? A new form of thought must no doubt be established to contain this sentence. But the process is endless; as rapidly as the forms multiply, borderline sentences will rise up to plague the classifier, who may eventually find, as a

---

[7] This rescue maneuver is my inference from Mr. Richards's position; *his* main aim is to debunk the monism of Mill's grammar.

result of his labors, that the number of forms precisely equals the number of sentences.

In raising this objection I have tentatively accepted the notion of "forms of thought," and merely questioned the practicability of their use by a critic. But the disconcerting proliferation of thought forms calls the whole theory into question. If there is a separate form for every thought, then the concept of "form" is identical with that of "thought," and we can dispense with one or the other. To look at the matter from another angle, let me press somewhat further the hypothetical meeting of man and tiger, attending to forms of thought. To an observer the tiger consists of certain sense data—color, texture, odor, shape, motion, sound—data related to each other in extremely complex ways, however simple and primitive an object the tiger may seem to the adult's highly integrated mind. The man is a similar complex. Both tiger and man are capable of receiving sensations from, say, the jungle around them, as well as from each other. And the jungle, like man and tiger, is a welter of surfaces, glints of light, disorderly movements, unmusical noises. In this tangle of sensation the man sees trees, plants, a tiger; but these *Gestalten* are not inherently *there;* they are arbitrary ways of breaking up the flux; arbitrary, that is, except that the man has in the past been rewarded for using them, to the extent that parts of his environment (e.g. the tiger) demand, with special persistence, recognition as separate things.[8] When the

---

[8] This view is, to the best of my knowledge, in accord with current perception theory. For instance: "perception is never a sure thing, never an absolute revelation of 'what is.' Rather, what we see is a prediction—our own personal construction designed to give us the best possible bet for carrying out our purposes in action. We make these bets on the basis of our past experience." W. H. Ittelson

man kicks the tiger, an exceedingly intricate shift takes place in the arrangement of sense data, a shift which is indistinguishable *in type* from the shifts which are occurring every millionth of a second. There has been a change; something has happened, but something is always happening, and it is man who separates one phenomenon from another, both by seeing and by naming. Our habits of sorting and classifying are so ingrained that we cannot describe or imagine things as they appear to the tiger, or in the infant's "blooming, buzzing confusion." The world in itself, the infant's world, is barren of form, without order, mere raw material for man's perceptual and verbal manipulation. The forms of thought, then, are not inherent in things as they are. There is no logical or ontological reason why, on some tiger-infested tropical island, a people could not see man and tiger as one entity, and give a single name to this "object." Then "I kick the tiger" might run, "The tigerman coalesces footwise," and "I see the tiger" could read, "The tigerman coalesces eyewise." Surely the two ideas are now of the same form, as are the two sentences.

In another section of *Interpretation in Teaching*,[9] Mr. Richards argues that communication depends on a sameness of experience —a uniformity offered from without and a uniformity as organized from within. His acceptance of "forms of thought" must depend on this "sameness," on a belief that experience affords common elements to all men. But if my analysis is correct, experience is not molded from without, except in so far as

---

and F. P. Kilpatrick, "Experiments in Perception," *Scientific American Reader* (New York, 1953), p. 581.

    [9] Page 68.

nature rewards certain of man's sorting responses to the passing show and punishes others. It is interesting to note that we may be led into a misconception partly by the very word "experience." A logician points out that " 'experience' itself is a relational term masquerading as a thing-name; x is an experience if and only if there is some y (the experiencer) which stands in the experience relation to x." [10] Ordinary language urges us to think of experience as a constant, offered with impartial sameness to all experiencers, rather than as an infinite series of relations of which no two need be alike.

The conception of experience as a series of relations is damaging also to Mr. Richards's claim that experience has "uniformity as organized from within," for it seems extremely improbable that any experiencer should ever stand in exactly the same relation to a field of perception as any other experiencer, or, indeed, that any man should see the same way twice. I do not wish to peddle a crippling subjectivism; communication does take place, and we must act most of the time as if there were uniformity of experience. At the same time it seems more accurate to speak behavioristically and say that men often *respond* similarly to similar fields of perception—respond similarly, that is, either in words or in action.

Neither the external world, then, nor our "experience" of it offers any ready-made forms of thought to the analyst who wishes to see style as the way in which ideas get into words. What nature does offer to experience, however, and experience to language, is a constant *formlessness*. Just as, in the exis-

[10] Charles W. Morris, "Foundations of the Theory of Signs," *International Encyclopedia of Unified Science*, I, 123.

tentialist view, man is confronted in his search for ethical order by the indifference of the universe, man in his search for perceptual order faces a chaotic world-stuff which gives no hints as to the proper method of sorting. But Camus calls the world's moral anarchy benign, in that it allows us to consider man the maker of his own morality, and the chaos pictured by modern psychologists has a parallel advantage: the perceiver, according to this theory, shapes the world by choosing from it whatever perceptual forms are most useful to him—though most often the choice is unconscious and inevitable. The unfriendly behavior of tigers may, to be sure, coerce him in his perceptual sorting, and his choice of perceptual forms largely governs his choice of linguistic categories, but the selections are initially free, in an important sense.

In these multifarious *ur*-choices, these preverbal and verbal pigeon-holings, style has its beginnings. If the critic is able to isolate and examine the most primitive choices which lie behind a work of prose, they can reveal to him the very roots of a writer's epistemology, the way in which he breaks up for manipulation the refractory surge of sensations which challenges all writers and all perceivers. In this Heraclitean flux, and not in the elusive forms of thought, is the common source of all perceptions, all sentences, all prose. The stream of experience is the background against which "choice" is a meaningful concept, in terms of which the phrase "*way* of saying *it*" makes sense, though "it" is no longer a variable. Form and content are truly separate if "content" is not bodiless ideas, but the formless world-stuff. And if such a hypothesis carries forward the analysis of style only a comfortless millimeter or so, at least it offers to that discipline a firm theoretical base, and a justification as well, inasmuch as it establishes an accessible and interesting connection between style and epistemology.

2

Before this hypothesis can be of use, however, it requires major refinement. The most obvious barrier to a fruitful consideration of these fundamental epistemic choices is the fact that most of them are irrevocably made for any given writer by the particular language he writes in. A James Joyce or a Gertrude Stein may reshuffle linguistic forms in an attempt to draw aside the curtain that English places between us and the world of psychic and physical phenomena, but most conventional writers permit English to govern their epistemologies, as do all who merely speak the language. In other words, writers in English deal with bare experience only as it is censored by their language; they manipulate linguistically a world which is already highly organized for them.

Take, for example, the question of grammatical case. In English, a language which, compared to its neighbors, is syntactically rigid and very slightly inflected, most contemporary linguists recognize two cases [11] (as opposed to the four, five, or six of earlier grammarians). Of these two, genitives are relatively uncommon, so that nearly all occurrences of nouns are in one

---

[11] "Contemporary" in a loose sense: Otto Jespersen, whose semi-notional approach to grammar has made him seem old-fashioned to many later linguists, is one who argues against more than two cases in English; *The Philosophy of Grammar* (London, 1924), pp. 173–86. Writers of the Fries-Trager-Smith era also favor a two-case system, as for example, Paul Roberts in *Understanding Grammar* (New York, 1954), pp. 39–40, and Donald Lloyd and Harry Warfel in *American English in Its Cultural Setting* (New York, 1956), pp. 241–42.

case. This limitation of cases means that a noun standing by itself, say "dog," calls attention merely to the animal of that name, and tells us nothing about it, not even that it is *not* a dog seen in an attitude of possession, since we have many constructions such as "hair of the dog" which express the genitive idea without recourse to the genitive case. The isolated word "dog's" names an animal *seen as owning something;* that is, it conveys a somewhat different idea. It also creates a different set of expectations; to say "dog" is probably to stimulate the question "What about a dog?"; but the word "dog's" leads to the question "Dog's what, and what about it?" Thus English offers the speaker or writer two different notions of a certain four-footed animal; it sees the canine beast in two different ways.

In French, by contrast, there is only one form of *chien.* That word in isolation tells nothing about the dog at all. At the atomic level of meaning English has two things where French has but one. When we turn to Latin, with its six cases, the difference becomes more obvious. To translate *canis* properly, we would have to use a term such as "dog-doing-something-or-having-something-predicated-of-it" (actually, a full translation would be much more complex even than this). *Canem* might be partially rendered "dog-being-acted-upon-or-seen-as-the-goal-of action." In Latin there is no conceivable way of expressing the English idea of "dog," untrammeled by ideas of position, agency, attitude, possession, mode of being perceived, and so forth. There is in Latin no symbol which is so free to be manipulated syntactically.

The writer in English, therefore, sees the universe through a verbal screen which divides it up less finely; classes are larger in English, because less subtly distinguished. What we conceive of as one thing, the writer of Latin must have conceived of, in some unquestioning, preverbal way, as six different things. These are the epistemic implications of case. The implications for style are equally significant: the importance of word order in English, the many possibilities of achieving emphasis in Latin by placement of a word, the greater dependence of the English writer on "function words." Epistemic differences of this sort run through the whole Indo-European family of languages, but within that family the similarities are more noticeable than the differences, and one must examine languages of other groups to find out how radically verbal environments can differ.

Benjamin Lee Whorf, a pioneer in metalinguistics, studied Western languages in juxtaposition with esoteric languages such as Hopi, and found that we treat the cosmos as much more segmented than do they—often artificially so.[12] We objectify time into a thing with boundaries and divisions instead of seeing it in terms of relations in lateness as Hopi does. We have "distributed nouns," such as "meat," "water," and "butter," whereas Hopi has none; nor does Hopi have abstract nouns. Evidently the Hopi language is in some sense closer to the raw material of perception than English is, with its complex and sophisticated system of categories.

It is notorious that Korzybski, Hayakawa, and other semanticists go further than Whorf, attacking Western languages for making inaccurate distinctions and concealing the functional

---

[12] *Language Thought, and Reality* (Cambridge, Mass., and New York, 1956), esp. "The Relation of Habitual Thought and Behavior to Language" and "Languages and Logic."

relationships of nature.[13] Supposedly, Indo-European language structure was responsible for our long slavery to Aristotelian philosophy and Newtonian physics [14] and is to blame for a good share of our present neuroses to boot. This criticism of ordinary language seems to me even more utopian than that leveled against it by the early positivists, and logically faulty as well. The semanticists use the very language which, according to them, hoodwinks us so severely to point out the fallacies of thought which it induces. Certainly a language which permits analysis of its own artificialities—which in effect transcends its own limitations—will suffice for most ordinary thinking.

Thus I find attacks on the cosmological limitations of English beside the point. What *is* relevant to the study of style is the fact that any language persuades its speakers to see the universe in certain set ways, to the exclusion of other ways. It thereby limits the possibilities of choice for any writer, and the student of style must be careful not to ascribe to an individual the epistemic bias of his language. A writer cannot escape the boundaries set by his tongue, except by creating new words, by uprooting normal syntax, or by building metaphors, each of which is a new ontological discovery. Yet, even short of these radical linguistic activities, an infinite number of meaningful choices remain to be made by the writer. A heavy dependence on abstraction, a peculiar use of the present tense, a habitual evocation of similarities through parallel structure, a tendency to place feelings in syntactical positions of agency, a trick of under-

[13] See, for example, "What Is Meant by Aristotelian Structure of Language?," in *Language, Meaning and Maturity,* ed. by S. I. Hayakawa (New York, 1954).

[14] According to this view it is not surprising that the Hopi have produced no Newton, but it is surprising that no Einstein has risen among the Pueblos.

playing causal words: any of these patterns of expression, when repeated with unusual frequency, is the sign of a habit of meaning, and thus of a persistent way of sorting out the phenomena of experience. And even single occurrences of linguistic oddities, especially in crucial places, can point to what might be called temporary epistemologies.

Here, then, is one way in which the term "style" is meaningful, one kind of *choice* which really exists for the author. This view does not, of course, represent an entirely new departure from conventional stylistics, even though my formulation has been elicited by the chaos of past criticism. Style as epistemic choice may be what John Middleton Murry has in mind when he says that "a true idiosyncrasy of style [is] the result of an author's success in compelling language to conform to his mode of experience." [15] It probably is what W. K. Wimsatt refers to when he calls style "the last and most detailed elaboration of meaning." [16] New or not, this approach to style has the advantage of being philosophically defensible, as well as the advantage of yielding results that have to do with the literary work as a whole, not merely with its (nonexistent) window dressing. Finally, the method which I suggest saves the study of style from having to rely *only* on those impressionistic, metaphorical judgments which have too often substituted for analysis: dignified, grand, plain, decorative, placid, exuberant, restrained, hard, and the whole tired assortment of epithets which name without explaining.[17]

---

[15] *The Problem of Style* (London, 1922), p. 23.

[16] *The Prose Style of Samuel Johnson* (New Haven, 1941), p. 63. Mr. Wimsatt is one critic who has fruitfully approached style in this way, both in this book and in *Philosophic Words* (New Haven, 1948).

[17] Such terms may be legitimately used to name habits of meaning which have

Yet this account of style is not complete. The naive, common-sense feeling that style is a *way* of saying *something* demands more than a cursory dismissal. For one thing, a discussion of style as epistemic choice can operate effectively only over wide areas of prose, where habitual kinds of choice become evident. There is little sense in comparing the epistemic decisions of a writer who is discussing a rowing match with those of a writer on Christian ideas of teleology. The very choice of subject matter precludes a large number of stylistic decisions: it can force the writer to be concrete or abstract, for instance. Thus the criticism of style requires a more manageable backdrop than the entire panorama of the world. If, as Wittgenstein says, "the world is the totality of facts, not of things," [18] perhaps individual facts, or combinations of them, will serve the purpose.

This position is the one that I propose to take, and I shall use the term "proposition" to describe what is expressed by sentences. As before, Mr. Richards's remarks will provide a convenient starting place for the argument. During a discussion. of logic [19] he lists these three sentences:

Mussolini is mortal.

Voltaire is witty.

Havelock Ellis is old.

A logician, he says, would claim that these sentences "express propositions of the same form," a contention which "is flagrantly not so." The first sentence, Mr. Richards says, means "Mussolini

---

been described specifically; see, for instance, Mr. Wimsatt's discussion of "plain" and its opposite, *Prose Style of Johnson*, p. 101. The more usual procedure, however, is to use them as if they had clear a priori meaning.

[18] Ludwig Wittgenstein, *Tractatus Logico-Philosophicus*, trans. by C. K. Ogden (London, 1922), p. 31.

[19] *Interpretation in Teaching*, p. 370.

will die sometime"; the second means "Voltaire makes remarks which cause in certain people, a peculiar pleasure, and in others a peculiar annoyance"; the third, "Havelock Ellis has lived through many years." These sentences show that "the similar adjectives stand for very different forms." Mr. Richards's analysis is revealing, and the particular logician he has in mind [20] *had* made the error of assuming that syntactical structure is a key to the structure of propositions. But Mr. Richards makes precisely the same error in implying that his *translations* of the first three sentences reveal the structure of the propositions they express, for he takes the translations as showing that the propositions are of different forms. And by what superior right is the sentence "Mussolini will die sometime" a better indication of propositional form than the sentence "Mussolini is mortal"? Or for that matter, why not other sentences, such as "Mussolini's life will end," or "Mussolini will not live forever"? If the first two sentences express the same proposition, then there are many other sentences which do so, and these sentences are of many syntactical forms. I see no way of picking one of such a group of sentences as *the* mirror of the proposition it expresses. [21]

The difficulty, of course, is that a "proposition," as Mr. Richards uses the term and as I wish to use it, has no form at all. The form of a proposition, like the forms of thought, is illusory, if I am right in what I take a proposition to be. It is the class of all sentences which are related to a fact or a cluster of facts in this way: if the fact (or cluster) exists, the sentences are all true; if the fact does not exist, the sentences are

---

[20] Susan Stebbing, *A Modern Introduction to Logic* (London, 1930), p. 51.

[21] The truth is, I think, that most logicians would say that Mr. Richards's *sentences* are of the same form, and not the propositions they express.

all false. In other words, they contain no parts which will not stand or fall with the fact. The process of determining, by observing facts, whether a sentence is true or false, is called "verification." [22] What may have led Mr. Richards to claim that his translations revealed the propositional forms which had been concealed by the original versions, is the fact that the restatements are more nearly descriptions of the facts which would go to *verify* the propositions involved.

Thus, for a sentence to express a proposition is for it to be a member of a group of sentences. But this class membership does not imply that a given sentence is one sub-form of a main propo-

[22] See A. J. Ayer, *Language, Truth and Logic,* rev. ed. (New York, 1946), pp. 13, 35, for a positivist's account of the criterion of verifiability. See also Alfred Tarski, "The Semantic Conception of Truth and the Foundations of Semantics," *Semantics and the Philosophy of Language* (Urbana, Ill., 1952), esp. pp. 15–17. According to Tarski, whose article is a classic in the field, the general definition of "truth" is a logical conjunction of all equivalences of the form "x is true, if and only if p," where "p" is any "true" sentence and "x" is the name of that sentence (i.e., that sentence in quotation marks). Tarski's definition seems to bypass propositions altogether by applying the term "true" to sentences only; and in view of the long dispute over propositions among logicians and philosophers, Tarski's move may be a wise application of Occam's razor. But it has the disadvantage of throwing out a term which is in common use by both philosophers and laymen, and the more severe disadvantage of leaving no term at all to describe that which sentences express. For these reasons I follow Ayer, *The Foundations of Empirical Knowledge* (London, 1940), pp. 100–1, in retaining the term. But I am made uncomfortable by an identification of "proposition" and "sentences which are true or false" (as in Wittgenstein, *Tractatus,* pp. 61–103), and more uncomfortable by a gentleman's agreement to use the term "proposition" while confessing ignorance as to its meaning. My own definition (which I have not seen elsewhere) is somewhat odd in that it requires us to think of a *class* of sentences as being true or false. But it jibes reasonably well with most technical usage, and has notable advantages for the study of style, the main one being that it places something between sentences and the facts, thus allowing meaningful talk of what sentences express (propositions) as well as of what they describe (facts).

sitional form. Rather, all members of the class have a most general form: the form "*x* is the case," or $f(x)$. And this form they have in common with *all* sentences, and with all propositions, for "the general propositional form is a variable." [23] This form distinguishes propositions from expletives, isolated words, commands, and so forth, none of which state that anything is the case, but it does not distinguish one proposition from another.

Propositions, then, offer a second locus for the analyst of style. Many sentences can express the same proposition; that is, they can be jointly verifiable by reference to the same fact. This is Bloomfield's contention when he states that "formally different utterances," though they always differ in meaning, may be equivalent "as to some partial phase of meaning." Equivalence covers "the phase of meaning which is observable indifferently by all persons," and "it is only the accompanying personal and social adjustments which differ." [24] These "adjustments" in language I would call "style," but it is worth noting again that they, as well as the root idea, are *meanings,* and not merely embellishment. Style is the hidden thoughts which accompany overt propositions; it is the highly general meanings which are implied by a writer's habitual methods of expressing propositions. Thus, as an aid to analyzing a writer's dissection of the entire universe, the critic may examine what the writer does with modest corners of that universe—that is, with particular facts and particular propositions.

Some theory such as the one I have been suggesting must be

[23] Wittgenstein, *Tractatus,* p. 103.
[24] *International Encyclopedia of Unified Science,* I, 253.

held by the modern critic who looks to style for insight into meaning, who believes that "the consideration of style is a consideration of complete meanings, and there is little of any importance that can be studied that is not a consideration of meanings." [25]

3

So far I have been outlining a theory of style which describes choices that I have called epistemic. These choices are important, for they are the critic's key to a writer's mode of experience. They show what sort of place the world is for him, what parts of it are significant or trivial. They show how he thinks, how he comes to know, how he imposes order on the ephemeral pandemonium of experience. These insights into a writer's world view are well worth pursuing, to whatever extent style can yield them. But an account of style which focuses on discursive content alone is only partial; style as it appears, for example, in the novel, I have left largely untouched. For the limits of speakable thought are not the boundaries of experience, or even of rational experience, and thoughts not included in the totality of verifiable propositions are nonetheless an integral part of style, as of knowledge. Thus argues Susanne Langer, who finds post-positivist man on "a tiny grammar-bound island" of human thought, in "the midst of a sea of feeling." [26] He wants to talk of good and evil, substance, beauty, and so forth, but whenever he does, he lapses into nonsense (according to the positivists). Mrs. Langer's method of egress from the narrow cage is well known. She calls symbolism of the

---

[25] Wanning, "Some Changes," p. 20.

[26] *Philosophy in a New Key* (New York: Mentor edition, 1948), pp. 70–71.

sort tolerated by radical empiricists "discursive," and claims that even beyond its limits there is a possibility of genuine semantic. This semantic she calls "presentational symbolism," because its symbols "are involved in a simultaneous, integral presentation." [27] Of this sort is the symbolism of single words, or cries, or music and the visual arts. It is a symbolism of emotional configurations, Mrs. Langer contends, for feelings have contours just as do thoughts, though of a different kind. They are static, grasped in sudden gestalts, rather than formed by gradual accretions of meaning. And to presentational symbolism belongs a large part of what we call "style," a part with which I have yet to deal.

Mrs. Langer says elsewhere,[28] "A statement is always a formulation of an idea, and every known fact or hypothesis or fancy takes its emotional value largely from the way it is presented and entertained." For "idea" my term is "proposition," and this substitution brings Mrs. Langer's statement into close parallelism with my analysis of varying descriptions of facts— but with this exception: her point is that one proposition may be expressed in many different *emotional* forms. The claim is incontestable; a large portion of the submerged meaning in prose is presentational, and the constant shaping of emotions is an always audible counterpoint to the melodic line of discursive thought. The presentational part of prose does not, of course, get communicated by a special set of symbols or by a code of emotive punctuation marks. It is buried in an exceedingly complex set of relationships among the same symbols which transmit the discursive meaning. These relationships are what Bloomfield referred to as "accompanying personal and social adjustments."

[27] *Ibid.*, p. 79.   [28] *Feeling and Form* (New York, 1953), p. 258.

Many critics see the emotional freight of literature as of primary importance, even in prose that is mainly discursive. Hence epigrams such as "Style is the man himself," or "Style is ingratiation." [29] Certainly the configurations of feeling which accompany any argument are vital in governing its reception by the reader. The writer must observe the amenities common to all human relationships, by "saying the right thing," as Kenneth Burke puts it, by showing himself a particular human being in a certain social relationship with his auditor.[30] Style adds the force of personality to the impersonal forces of logic and evidence, and is thus deeply involved in the business of persuasion. Students of rhetoric since Plato have been largely concerned, at one or another level of sophistication, with analyzing the role of emotion in inducing agreement, and with the methods of embodying it in writing.

But an analysis of tone, distance, dramatic situation, and the rest, solely as ways of persuading, is only a partial analysis, and one which can lead to the damaging distrust of rhetoric as tricky and insidious. Emotion enters prose not only as disguises for slipping into the reader's confidence, but as sheer expression of self. Complete honesty demands that the writer not only state his ideas accurately, but also take an emotional stance. A proposition is never held altogether dispassionately, nor can it be expressed without some indication of feeling (except in the artificial languages of logic and mathematics, where symbols and structural patterns have no connotations, no psychic contexts). This being so, the writer must either recreate in prose

---

[29] Kenneth Burke, *Permanence and Change* (New York, 1935), p. 71.
[30] See Reuben Arthur Brower, *The Fields of Light* (New York, 1951), chap. 1, for this view of tone.

the emotional concomitants of his thinking, or be in some degree unfaithful to himself. To acknowledge the expressive value of tone, however, is not to say that it is isolated from the persuasive value. When a writer such as Newman creates a full picture of the frame of mind in which he approaches a problem and reader, he is being honest, certainly, but his self-revelation may have the effect of persuading the reader to follow the same emotional path. With Arnold and many other writers the two uses of tone are even more inextricably fused. Arnold argues for a temper of mind, rather than for a set of specific doctrines. In his prose, therefore, tone *is* the argument, in large measure: ingratiation and personality become one, for the case stands or falls depending on whether Arnold's feelings and attitudes are attractive to his readers.[31] His use of language is presentational in that a full understanding of his prose depends on a grasp of the emotional pattern which it presents.

Feeling enters discursive prose, then, as expression and as persuasion. In addition there is a third way, I think, which is almost beyond the power of language to describe. A sentence, at its inception, raises questions rather than answering them. The first word or two may limit the field of possible things-to-be-said, but they do not really transmit information. They may name something, or set an attitude toward something, or indicate a shift in direction from a previous sentence, but they always give rise to questions such as "What about it?" or "What am I to think of in that way?" These demands for completion of a sequence are of course subverbal; they are the vaguest sort of

[31] I am indebted for this notion to John Holloway, *The Victorian Sage* (London, 1953), p. 207.

dissatisfaction with suspended thought, with a rational process not properly concluded. As the sentence progresses some of the demands are satisfied, others deferred, others complicated, and meanwhile new ones are created. But with the end of the sentence comes a kind of balance which results from something having been *said*. There may be a new set of indefinite expectations which remain for future sentences to gratify or disappoint, but one circle is completed, one temporary equilibrium gained. The very act of predication is an emotional act, with rhythms of its own. To state something is first to create imbalance, curiosity, where previously there was nothing, and then to bring about a new balance. So prose builds on the emotional force of coming to know, of pinning down part of what has previously been formless and resolving the tensions which exist between the human organism and unstructured experience. Mrs. Langer speaks of the

> feeling that naturally inheres in studious thinking, the growing intensity of a problem as it becomes more and more complex, and at the same time more definite and "thinkable," until the demand for answer is urgent, touched with impatience; the holding back of assent as the explanation is prepared; the cadential feeling of solution, and the expansion of consciousness in new knowledge.[32]

To emotion, then, as well as to epistemic choice, the stylistic critic must turn his attention. This part of the study is and always has been particularly enticing, perhaps because the individual character of a writer emerges with special clarity in the patterns of feeling which are habitual with him. The

---

[32] *Feeling and Form*, p. 302.

epistemic part of style, moreover—a writer's method of dissecting the universe, as expressed by the infinite number of choices he makes—is likely to seem indistinguishable from what he overtly *says*. Yet this is all the more reason for pursuing stylistic meaning through the maze of surface meaning. That which is not immediately obvious may be just as central to the spirit of the writer, and therefore just as valuable to know, as that which starts up unbidden from the page. And, finally, it should be said that a dichotomy between thought and emotion, though useful, is artificial. A writer's characteristic way of manipulating experience is organically related to his feelings about coming to know; his attitude toward the reader and toward the process of communicating is also part of the whole.

The view of style which I have been outlining clearly takes prose as a serious literary venture. What Leo Spitzer says of the purely imaginative forms is also true of good discursive prose: "the lifeblood of the poetic creation is everywhere the same, whether we tap the organism at 'language' or 'ideas,' at 'plot' or at 'composition.'"[33] This rather mystical theory makes good sense if "lifeblood" is translatable to "modes of experience and habits of feeling." Spitzer's dictum means only that a work of prose can be self-consistent just as a good poem is, its fabric all of a piece. Such a view is the direct antithesis of the older one, which saw style as sugar-coating; if my hypothesis is legitimate, style is just as useful a key to total meaning as is any other element. For this reason, and for no other, it is worth studying: to say something about style is to contribute fresh insight into the artistic contours of the work as a whole.

---

[33] *Linguistics and Literary History* (Princeton, 1948), p. 18.

Albrecht B. Strauss

On Smollett's Language : A Paragraph
In *Ferdinand Count Fathom*

Few modern readers, I suspect, will quarrel with George
Saintsbury's judgment that *Ferdinand Count Fathom* is
"Smollett's least good novel," [1] and there are likely to be even
fewer who would deny that its concluding pages are the least
successful part of an unsuccessful book. As happens time and
time again in Smollett's works, the mood set at the beginning
has not been sustained, the promise of the brilliant opening
chapters has not been kept. Long before we have reached the
novel's denouement, the savage irony of the battlefield scenes
(and there is nothing more scathing in all of Smollett) has
been dissipated, and by the time we near the end all we are
left with is a curious mélange of incongruous fairy tale material
and conventional Gothic claptrap, as embarrassing to the reader
as one fondly hopes it must have been to the writer. Indeed,

[1] *The Works of Tobias Smollett,* ed. by George Saintsbury (12 vols., London,
1899–1900), VIII, xviii. All citations of Smollett in my text are from this edition.
However, in the absence of a reliable modern edition, I have compared their text
with that of the same passages in the original editions and silently restored earlier
readings whenever I have found significant variants. The following abbreviations
are used: *RR = Roderick Random; PP = Peregrine Pickle; FF = Ferdinand Count
Fathom; LG = Sir Launcelot Greaves; HC = Humphry Clinker.*

Smollett's manifest eagerness to hurry the novel to a conclusion would suggest that he was not unaware of having been caught out of his depth.

And yet, however unsatisfactory the final chapters of *Ferdinand Count Fathom* may seem, they are by no means unrepresentative. An artist's failures, it has sometimes been argued, are more revealing than his successes. Whether this be true or not, there can be no question that his peculiar mannerisms and habitual techniques may well stand out more starkly in a novelist's less finished works than they do in his triumphs. No apologies should thus be needed for having selected as a point of departure for my discussion a paragraph which, coming as it does from the final part of *Ferdinand Count Fathom,* certainly does not represent Smollett at his best.

I

The passage I have chosen is taken from Chapter 64, and runs as follows:

> This powerful shock aroused his faculties; a cold sweat bedewed his forehead; his knees began to totter; he dropped upon the floor, and throwing his arms around her, cried, "O nature! O Serafina! Merciful Providence! thy ways are past finding out." So saying, he fell upon her neck, and wept aloud. The tears of sympathetic joy trickled down her snowy bosom, that heaved with rapture inexpressible. Renaldo's eyes poured forth the briny stream. The cheeks of Madam Clement were not dry in this conjuncture; she kneeled by Serafina, kissed her with all the eagerness of maternal affection, and with uplifted hands adored the Power that preordained this blessed event. The clergyman

and doctor intimately shared the general transport; and as for Joshua, the drops of true benevolence flowed from his eyes, like the oil on Aaron's beard, while he skipped about the room in an awkward ecstasy, and in a voice resembling the hoarse notes of the long-eared tribe, cried, "O father Abraham! such a moving scene hath not been acted since Joseph disclosed himself unto his brethren in Egypt."   (*FF*, II, 215-16)

Described here is the emotional impact of the familiar recognition scene, a plot device of venerable antiquity which, as part of the picaresque and dramatic heritage that Smollett shared with Fielding, has found its way into all but one of Smollett's five novels. In this particular instance, one Don Diego de Zelos, a fiery Castilian nobleman, has just been reunited with a daughter whom he had not only thought dead, but for whose rash poisoning he had bitterly blamed himself. A few pages earlier, in a ghoulish midnight setting that has often been said to anticipate "Monk" Lewis and Mrs. Radcliffe, Don Diego's young friend and benefactor, Renaldo, had recovered his Monimia, supposedly dead by the machinations of the fiendish Fathom. Now, this same Monimia has turned out to be identical with Don Diego's long-lost daughter, Serafina. Surprise, in short, is heaped upon surprise, and indeed the end is not yet. It is all most tiresome, and there would be no excuse for rehearsing these confusing details if they did not supply the necessary background for a paragraph that, whatever its literary merits, admirably illustrates some aspects of Smollett's manner.

Take, for example, the opening sentence. Smollett is clearly straining hard to suggest a state of intense emotion. Somehow he will have to convey Don Diego's mingled feelings of relief, incredulity, fondness, gratitude, and shock. In the paragraph preceding the one we are considering he had made a half-hearted attempt to solve his problem by resorting to an analogy. The Castilian, he had said, was like a parent who "unexpectedly retrieves a darling child from the engulfing billows or devouring flame." Then he had back-tracked to recall the anguish suffered by the Don in the years since the supposed murder. But Smollett is not the man to linger over subtle Jamesian analyses of states of feeling. Like Fielding and Dickens, he is committed to describing emotional life mainly by its external manifestations. And so he now gives us an account of the Don's reflexes, or rather the lack thereof. The Don, we are informed, "started out, nor did he lift an hand in token of surprise; he moved not from the spot on which he stood; but, riveting his eyes to those of the lovely phantom, remained without motion." Such absolute immobility, however, cannot be maintained for long, and when Monimia approaches to exclaim plaintively "May I yet call you father?" something in the Don gives way. The result is the sentence with which our paragraph begins: "The powerful shock aroused his faculties; a cold sweat bedewed his forehead; his knees began to totter; he dropped upon the floor, and throwing his arms around her, cried, 'O nature! O Serafina! Merciful Providence! thy ways are past finding out.'"

The technique used here to impress us with the keenness of the Don's feelings is not uncommon in the eighteenth-century novel. Professor Ian Watt has recently noticed it in *Tom Jones*. "Fielding's use of . . . hackneyed hyperboles to vouch for the intensity of the emotions of his characters," he writes, "underlines the price that he pays for his comic approach: it denies him a convincing and continuous access to the inner life of his characters, so that whenever he has to exhibit their emotional life, he can only do it externally by making them have exaggerated physical reactions." [2] Much the same, of course, holds true of Smollett. One remembers, for instance, a passage from *Roderick Random,* in which Roderick, having been made insanely jealous by Narcissa's complaisance to a nobleman, vents his fury on the long-suffering Strap: "It set all my passions into a new ferment, I swore horrible oaths without meaning or application, I foamed at the mouth, kicked the chairs about the room, and played abundance of mad pranks, that frightened my friend almost out of his senses. At length my transport subsided, I became melancholy, and wept insensibly" (*RR,* III, 109). What does seem peculiar to Smollett, however, is a tendency to lapse into ready-made formulas whenever the occasion for describing strong emotions arises. Whether the emotion be rapture or distress, anger or terror, Smollett always has a readily available repertoire of descriptive phrases to fall back upon. To adapt these to a particular situation all he needs do is to rearrange or embroider. It is a technique that recalls the practice of epic poets.

But let me illustrate. Characteristically perhaps, no emotion is more regularly described in Smollett's novels than fear. The basic formula for the portrayal of this emotion appears to consist of the following three elements found in an account of Davy Dawdle's terror in *Sir Launcelot Greaves:* "His hair bristled up, his teeth chattered, and his knees knocked" (*LG,* p. 203). Slightly rearranged, this triad occurs earlier in the same

---

[2] *The Rise of the Novel* (London, 1957), p. 274.

novel in a description of Captain Crowe's fear: "This no sooner saluted his view," we learn, "than his hair bristled up, his knees began to knock, and his teeth to chatter" (*LG,* p. 75). To be sure, there are minor variants of the pattern, in which one or two different elements have been substituted for one of those I have arbitrarily called the basic ones. Thus, we hear of Fathom finding himself in an isolated cottage with nothing but a still warm corpse to keep him company: "Then his heart began to palpitate, his hair to bristle up, and his knees to totter" (*FF,* I, 118), and the same Fathom, being locked up in Wilhelmina's closet, is described in the following terms: "He trembled at every joint, the sweat trickled down his forehead, his teeth began to chatter, his hair to stand on end" (*FF,* I, 69). Finally, in the following more elaborate specimen describing Trunnion's terror upon beholding a "vision," we find the three basic elements supplemented with a fourth: "a cold sweat bedewed his limbs, his knees knocked together, his hair bristled up, and the remains of his teeth were shattered to pieces in the convulsive vibrations of his jaws" (*PP,* I, 46).

Also, of course, there are more radical variants which share no more than one element with those listed thus far. A farmer's fear in *Roderick Random,* for instance, takes the following form: "his hair erect, his eyes staring, his nostrils dilated, and his mouth wide open" (*RR,* II, 129–30); and Humphry's terror at an apparition has him running into the kitchen "with his hair standing on end, staring wildly, and deprived of utterance" (*HC,* II, 98). All these efforts to describe the physical effects of fear culminate in this passage, the most ornate of its kind I have found in Smollett's novels: frightened by Sir Launcelot's

forbidding appearance and even more by his threatening manner, Ferret, we read, is reduced "to a temporary privation of
all his faculties. His eyes retired within their sockets; his com-
plexion, which was naturally of a copper hue, now shifted to a
leaden colour; his teeth began to chatter; and all his limbs were
agitated by a sudden palsy" (*LG,* p. 17).

Clearly, such a method has serious drawbacks. While emi-
nently serviceable for comic ends, it proves totally inadequate
when used in an uncomical context. Now, it is true, of course,
that both fear and pain are almost always comic in Smollett.
Other emotions, however, are obviously not; and because he is
committed to the method we have been examining, Smollett
is ill-equipped to deal with them. It is not only that the physical
reactions Smollett manipulates are so crude as to be incapable of
doing justice to finer shades of feeling, there is also the inherent
difficulty of drawing the line between the external manifestations of one kind of emotion and those of another. Thus, when
he seeks to describe Peregrine's jealousy at a ball, all Smollett
can say is, "The sweat ran down his forehead in a stream,
the colour vanished from his cheeks, his knees began to totter,
and his eyesight to fail" (*PP,* IV, 17); and when he attempts to
convey Tunley's fury—in what, to be sure, is a comic passage—
he is reduced to writing "his nostrils were dilated more than
one-half beyond their natural capacity, his eyes rolled, his teeth
chattered, he snored in breathing as if he had been oppressed
by the nightmare, and streams of sweat flowed down each side
of his forehead" (*PP,* I, 205). Taken out of context, both
passages could just as easily be thought to describe fear as
jealousy, shock as indignation. The instrument is simply not

delicate enough to register and distinguish among the various kinds of emotional pressure; and when we read that "Mr. Bramble no sooner received this reply, than his eyes began to glisten, his face grew pale, and his teeth chattered" (*HC,* I, 39), all we really know is that Bramble is violently moved—whether by fear or anger, shock or envy, we are left to glean from the context.

Similarly, nothing in the opening sentences of the paragraph from *Ferdinand Count Fathom* does so much as hint at the complexity of Don Diego's emotions. "The powerful shock aroused his faculties; a cold sweat bedewed his forehead; his knees began to totter": these are all stock phrases which we have previously encountered in radically different contexts and which might describe any number of different sentiments. Smollett's formulaic method of characterizing emotions is thus of only limited usefulness. It does, as I have said, lend itself admirably to comedy: the accounts of Trunnion's and Ferret's panic are ample proof of that. But when it comes to describing uncomical emotions, the method breaks down. Even if he had been far more resourceful in the observation and delineation of external manifestations of emotional life, Smollett would presumably have been unable to do justice to the state of Don Diego's mind. By limiting himself to a handful of stereotyped details, he makes his failure a foregone conclusion. Smollett's stylistic equipment, in short, cannot cope with the task it has been set here.

2

But, of course, we do not look to Smollett for pathos. What we prize him for, above all else, is his boisterous, farcical humor;

and it is only proper, therefore, before we consider the diction of our paragraph, to glance for a moment at the concluding portion of the passage which, in its own way, is as representative of Smollett's comic vein as the beginning one is of his attempts at pathos. The dramatically conceived tableau is rounded out, one recalls, with the following sentence: "and as for Joshua, the drops of true benevolence flowed from his eyes, like the oil on Aaron's beard, while he skipped about the room in an awkward ecstasy, and in a voice resembling the hoarse notes of the long-eared tribe, cried, 'O father Abraham! such a moving scene hath not been acted since Joseph disclosed himself unto his brethren in Egypt.'"

The technique is characteristically Smollettian. Having circumstantially created an atmosphere charged with sentiment, Smollett (as Byron might have done) undercuts the mood by the introduction of a ludicrous detail. Much the same device is used, for example, in a recognition scene between Roderick Random and Strap. When Roderick, currently a semi-starved French soldier, confronts Strap, now transformed into the elegant Monsieur d'Estrapes, the former schoolmate, we are told, "leaped upon me in a transport of joy, hung about my neck, kissed me from ear to ear, and blubbered like a great schoolboy who has been whipt" (*RR*, II, 183). Similarly, what might have become an intensely affecting reunion between old Matthew Bramble and Rear-Admiral Balderick, a companion of his youth now "metamorphosed into an old man, with a wooden leg and a weather-beaten face," is quickly diverted into farce when the Admiral—so Bramble reports—"in saluting me, . . . thrust the spring of his spectacles into my eye, and, at the same time, set his wooden stump upon my gouty toe; an attack that made me shed tears in sad earnest" (*HC,* I, 70–71). It is as though deep down Smollett feared sentiment, as though, just because he was inclined that way, he were unwilling to indulge himself in something so unmanly. "My uncle and he," reports Melford of Bramble and Quin, "are perfectly agreed in their estimate of life, which, Quin says, would stink in his nostrils, if he did not steep it in claret" (*HC,* I, 65). Smollett must laugh so as to keep from weeping.

And the figure of Joshua skipping about the room in "an awkward ecstasy" is, of course, sufficiently laughable. Unlike the other figures in our tableau, Joshua has been conceived in comic terms from the start. A "benevolent Israelite" (*FF,* II, 68) he may be and thus, in the management of Renaldo's affairs, an appropriately named successor to the wicked Fathom—a villain who had looked upon England "as the Canaan of all able adventurers" (*FF,* I, 106), and who, while still in Boulogne, had "surveyed the neighbouring coast of England with fond and longing eyes, like another Moses, reconnoitring the land of Canaan from the top of Mount Pisgah" (*FF,* I, 177). But, for all that he constitutes a notable departure from the stereotype Jew of English literature, some of the oddities of the traditional Jewish stage villain still cling to him. Upon first approaching him to plead for a loan, Renaldo, already frightened by his preconceptions about Jews, is thrown into "disorder and affliction" by "the looks of the Jew, who . . . pulled down his eyebrows, which were surprisingly black and bushy, so as, in appearance, totally to extinguish his vision" (*FF,* II, 66). Later, when Fathom had eloquently reinforced Renaldo's suit by drawing "a most pathetic picture of his distress," "the Jew listened attentively for some time; then his eyebrows began to rise and fall alternately; he coughed, sneezed, and winking hard, 'I'm plagued,' said he, 'with a salt rheum that trickles from my eyes without intermission' " (*FF*, II, 66–67). Black and bushy eyebrows, traditionally a token of Jewish villainy, have thus been made over into an emblem of the Jew's benevolence, or, at any rate, they have become closely allied with Joshua's propensity to vent his compassion in tears. And, indeed, it is his readiness to shed tears of sympathy that becomes the *leitmotiv* which is regularly sounded whenever the Jew appears. Renaldo's first call after returning to England from the Court of Vienna is on "the generous Jew, whose rheum," we are told, "distilled very plentifully at his approach" (*FF*, II, 191). By the time we reach our passage, we have come to take it for granted that, given the proper provocation, "drops of true benevolence" will readily stream from Joshua's eyes.

If it did nothing else, his having become associated with a *leitmotiv* would mark Joshua as the Jonsonian humor character that he is. No more than Fielding is Smollett interested in numbering the streaks of the tulip: his characters, for all their manifest eccentricities, are always types rather than individuals. Commodore Trunnion is not a kindly man who happens to have spent his life at sea, but an old tar who also happens to be warm-hearted; and Tabitha Bramble is not an avaricious female who happens to be unmarried, but a predatory spinster about whose femininity, as a matter of fact, we may entertain considerable doubts. The eccentricities of both are merely typical traits heightened to grotesque proportions. In much the same way, I think, Joshua must not be thought of as one Joshua Manasseh, a Jew with bushy black eyebrows and a pretended "salt rheum" who happens to be surprisingly generous, but as the type of the benevolent Israelite. Whatever Smollett's motives may have been for wanting to do so in 1753, the year of the Jewish Naturalization Act, he is clearly attempting to replace one generic figure—that of Isaac Rapine, the unsavory usurer in *Roderick Random*—with another, infinitely more appealing one.

As such a type figure, Joshua can be expected to manifest his typicality whenever he appears; and we have already seen that his pretended "salt rheum" may be thought of as a generic trait. But, as every reader of Smollett knows, the device most commonly used to assign characters to their social and racial origins is idiom. Smollett's soldiers and sailors, his lawyers and physicians, his Welshmen and Yorkshiremen all tend to express themselves in the language peculiar to their profession or place of origin, and, in fact, much of Smollett's humor derives either from the excessive technicality of their jargon or, more often perhaps, from the application of that jargon to incongruous subjects. A passage from *Roderick Random,* describing a coach ride in the early morning darkness, is representative: "The first five minutes passed in a general silence, when, all of a sudden, the coach heeling to one side, a boisterous voice pronounced, 'To the right and left, cover your flanks, damme! whiz!' I easily discovered by the tone and matter of this exclamation, that it was uttered by a son of Mars; neither was it hard to conceive the profession of another person who sat opposite to me, and observed, that we ought to have been well satisfied of the security before we entered upon the premises" (*RR*, III, 62–63). As so often in Smollett, professional idiom has here been used for comic identification; and we need but recall the Bowlings and Trunnions, the Tom Clarkes and Dr. Lindens, the Morgans and Dolly Cowslips to realize how thoroughly Smollett was to exploit the humorous possibilities of the device. Nor is this to be wondered at. Precluded by his method from dealing with the inner man and restricted to the external, Smollett was virtually driven into drawing upon speech as one of the main sources of characterization and humor —not only because this is the way it had been used by the dramatists, but also because if a man is to be exhibited by externals only, idiom will be one of the few devices a writer can work with.

It might thus have been predicted that when Joshua would be heard from, he should first apostrophize one of the patriarchs and then express his delight by producing a pertinent Biblical parallel. In so doing, of course, he is being *the* Jew rather than a philanthropic individual. As a matter of fact, the only curious thing is that he has not resorted to Biblical language before this. But then, even on Smollett's terms, the figure of Joshua is hardly a rounded portrait: up to this point, one suspects, Smollett has taken comparatively few pains with it. In our passage, however, he works with greater deliberation. In addition to the Biblical exclamation, he now contrives two similes for Joshua, both of which are conditioned by the man's Jewishness: the flow of Joshua's tears, it will be remembered, is compared to that of the "oil on Aaron's beard," and the voice in which he speaks is said to resemble "the hoarse notes of the long-eared tribe."

To start with the second: critics have recently made much of a tendency among eighteenth-century writers in general and Smollett in particular to see man as an animal. V. S. Pritchett, for instance, in a brilliant essay on "The Shocking Surgeon," urges us to study the engravings Rowlandson did for *Humphry Clinker* if we wish to "see Smollett come into focus once more": here are to be found, he says, not human beings, but "lumps of animal horror or stupidity." "To Rowlandson," writes Pritchett, "the human race are cattle or swine, a reeking fat-stock done up in ribbons or breeches, which has got into coffee-houses, beds and drawing-rooms." [3] And the artist's world, he suggests, faithfully mirrors that of Smollett. Walter Allen, in *The English Novel*, makes much the same observation: "Characters in Smollett," he says, "have become grotesque objects and, deprived of their human appearances, turned into animals or insects, they are deprived of their humanity." [4] Finally, Alan D. McKillop, in his recent *The Early Masters of English Fiction*, repeatedly alludes to Smollett's use of "the device of animal caricature." [5]

Ample support for all these observations may certainly be found in specific passages associating society with the animal kingdom, in the entire tenor of Smollett's treatment of individuals as gross, instinct-ridden brutes, and, above all perhaps, in the frequent resort to animal imagery as an instrument for characterization. One remembers, for example, the Apologue

[3] *The Living Novel* (New York, 1947), pp. 32–33.
[4] *English Novel* (New York, 1957), p. 63.
[5] *Early Masters* (Lawrence, Kansas, 1956), pp. 153, 159.

to *Roderick Random,* which links a soldier to a bear, a physician to an ass, and a statesman to an owl (*RR,* I, xlv–xlvi); and there is a striking passage in *Ferdinand Count Fathom* which explicitly spells out Smollett's sardonic view of society:

He had formerly imagined [we are told of Fathom], but was now fully persuaded, that the sons of men preyed upon one another, and such was the end and condition of their being. Among the principal figures of life, he observed few or no characters that did not bear a strong analogy to the savage tyrants of the wood. One resembled a tiger in fury and rapaciousness; a second prowled about like an hungry wolf, seeking whom he might devour; a third acted the part of a jackal, in beating the bush for game to his voracious employer; and a fourth imitated the wily fox, in practising a thousand crafty ambuscades for the destruction of the ignorant and unwary. (*FF,* I, 54–55)

It is thoroughly in keeping with such a vision, moreover, that Lavement, the London apothecary, should discover an affinity to a baboon (*RR,* I, 131–32), that Sir Launcelot's Trulliber-like squire, Timothy Crabshaw, is found to be endowed with "small glimmering eyes" which resemble "those of the Hampshire porker, that turns up the soil with his projecting snout" (*LG,* p. 12), and that even Lismahago will at various times be compared with a grasshopper (*HC,* II, 13), a hedgehog, a mule, an elephant (*HC,* II, 161), a squirrel (*HC,* II, 162), and a tame bear (*HC,* II, 170). Indeed, there are even subtler ways in which Smollett sets about dehumanizing his characters. To take just one example: in sneering at *nouveau riche* yeomen, he artfully draws on animal imagery to intimate that the women folk have been assimilated to the cattle they have for so long taken care of: "their wives and daughters," he writes, "appeared in their jewels, their silks, and their satins, their negligees and trollopees; their clumsy shanks, like so many shins of beef, were cased in silk hose and embroidered slippers; their raw red fingers, gross as the pipes of a chamber organ, which had been employed in milking the cows, in twirling the mop or churn-staff, being adorned with diamonds, were taught to thrum the pandola, and even to touch the keys of the harpsichord!" (*LG,* p. 27). Clearly, these are not women, but coarse animals grotesquely masquerading as human beings.

Upon occasion, the propensity to think of men as beasts and to associate human with animal traits may even generate meaningful image patterns. Consider, for example, the animal images used in connection with what might be called the domestication of Trunnion. Long before Mrs. Grizzle has conceived marital designs on the hapless Commodore, Trunnion has been firmly associated with a wooden lion. At the celebration of Gamaliel Pickle's wedding, Trunnion's imperturbability, we are told, "provoked the mirth of a certain wag, who, addressing himself to the lieutenant, asked whether that was the commodore himself, or the wooden lion that used to stand at his gate? An image," Smollett remarks, "to which, it must be owned, Mr. Trunnion's person bore no faint resemblance" (*PP,* I, 25). Shortly after the beginning of her "campaign," at the moment when Mrs. Grizzle has artfully persuaded the reluctant Commodore to part with three black hairs which the now pregnant Mrs. Pickle capriciously desires to pluck from his beard, a new association, this one with a reluctant bear, is established. In a passage that bodes ill for his future, we learn that Trunnion "at last complied, and was conducted to the scene like a victim to the altar by the exulting priests, or rather growling like a reluctant bear, when he is led to the stake amidst the shouts and cries of butchers and their dogs" (*PP*, I, 35).

And to the altar, of course, Trunnion is destined to go, though by a somewhat circuitous route. No sooner are they married than the redoubtable Mrs. Grizzle undertakes to reform "the whole economy of the garrison," and all the unhappy Commodore gains by offering forcible opposition is a hammer blow from a carpenter "by which the sight of his remaining eye was grievously endangered" (*PP*, I, 62). Once again, the imagery clearly reflects Trunnion's helplessness. Though the workmen who had assaulted him in ignorance of his quality demean themselves to ask forgiveness, the Commodore, "far from being satisfied with this apology," "began to storm with incredible vociferation, like a lion roaring in the toil, pouring forth innumerable oaths and execrations" (*PP*, I, 63). His fury, however, proves unavailing; and when the new Mrs. Trunnion not only brazenly sides with the workmen, but even prevails upon Hatchway and Pipes to join her in doing so, Trunnion's subjection is complete. Utterly humbled, "he was committed to the care of Pipes, by whom he was led about the house like a blind bear growling for prey, while his industrious yoke-fellow executed every circumstance of the plan she had projected" (*PP*, I, 64). The wooden lion has thus become a lion roaring in the toils, the reluctant bear a blinded one.

But while overpowered, Trunnion is by no means defeated, and two further animal images, that of a mule and that of a tortoise, suggests the Commodore's new station in life. After three months of marriage, Smollett reports, Trunnion was a "thorough-paced husband." "Not," he adds, "that his obstinacy was extinguished, though overcome; in some things he was as inflexible and mulish as ever; but then he durst not kick so openly, and was reduced to the necessity of being passive in his resentments" (*PP*, I, 65). His newly-developed mulishness is exemplified by Trunnion's stubborn refusal to heed his wife's pleas for a coach and six: unmoved by her eloquence, he "seemed to retire within himself, like a tortoise when attacked, that shrinks within its shell, and silently endured the scourge of her reproaches, without seeming sensible of the smart" (*PP*, I, 66). To be sure, his wife's alleged pregnancy is presently to put an end to his resolution; but his strategy presumably survives this interlude. At one time a lion and a bear, he has now been transformed into a mule and a tortoise. But after all, he still has his rebellious moments, the bear in him is not completely eradicated, and there is one final passage, several chapters later, in which Smollett reverts to the bear image. Comparing Trunnion's marriage with Pickle's, he says, "Trunnion's subjection was like that of a bear, chequered with fits of surliness and rage; whereas Pickle bore the yoke like an ox, without repining" (*PP*, I, 140).

Image patterns of the sort we have just traced are fairly rare in Smollett, and it is therefore all the more significant, I think, that when one does occur, it should consist of animal images. Its presence brings home to us how natural it was for Smollett's comic vision to focus on man's affinity with various species of animals, and, so far as our paragraph is concerned, it impresses us with the fact that Smollett is only following his habitual bent when he associates Joshua's bellowing with "the hoarse notes" of asses. But why "the long-eared tribe"? Is this merely a conventional eighteenth-century periphrasis? Or is Smollett playing on the word "tribe" with its Jewish overtones? And finally, does he have any particular reason for associating the voice of a Jew with the braying of an ass?

The answer to all these questions may be found, I submit, in a brief episode in *Peregrine Pickle,* where, as he travels through the Lowlands in a diligence, Peregrine's tutor, Jolter, gets himself involved in a heated philological argument with a Rotterdam Jew. Their exchange culminates in Jolter's ironic question, "to which of the tribes the Jew thought he belonged." The Jew's reply, made "with a most significant grin," is, "To the tribe of Issachar!" (*PP,* II, 130). As H. R. S. van der Veen has pointed out,[6] the joke here is evidently the allusion to Jacob's blessing in Genesis 49.14, "Issachar is a strong ass." Van der Veen takes the whole affair to be proof of Smollett's intimate knowledge of the Bible. In any case, however, it seems at least plausible that when he wrote the conclusion of *Ferdinand Count Fathom* some two years after he composed the above episode in *Peregrine Pickle,* Smollett remembered the verse he had previously alluded to and allowed his memory of it to guide his pen. "The hoarse notes of the long-eared tribe" would then be a kind of private joke, the sort of joke

[6] *Jewish Characters in Eighteenth Century English Fiction and Drama* (Groningen, 1935), p. 46.

one might expect of a writer who, as Giorgio Melchiori has recently argued, anticipates in the letters of Winifred Jenkins the verbal ingenuity of *Finnegans Wake*.[7]

It remains for us to consider the first simile in our sentence, that which associates Joshua's tears with "the oil on Aaron's beard." The allusion is evidently to the second verse of Psalm 133, where social harmony is compared with "the precious ointment upon the head, that ran down upon the beard, even Aaron's beard: that went down to the skirts of his garments." I do not know how erudite this reference is; its being listed in the *Oxford Dictionary of Quotations* might indicate that it is not extraordinarily so. At any rate, it is clear that the allusion is singularly appropriate both to the person, a Jew, and to the situation, one in which, to quote Psalm 133 again, "brethren . . . dwell together in unity."

Smollett's similes and metaphors, one should add, are not always so fresh. He is often content to fall back upon a thoroughly conventional figure—as when Renaldo's Serafina is compared to "a precious jewel locked up in a casket, which the owner alone has an opportunity to contemplate" (*FF*, II, 260), or when Emilia's appearance is said to have acted upon Peregrine's imagination "like a spark of fire that falls among gunpowder" (*PP*, I, 152). But particularly in his later works, where Smollett's imagination seems to work increasingly through and with images, homely and vivid touches abound. "He found it barely practicable," we hear of Fathom's difficulties in a coach, "to insinuate himself sidelong between a corpulent quaker and a fat Wapping landlady, in which attitude he

<hr>

[7] *The Tightrope Walkers* (London, 1956), pp. 46–49.

stuck fast, like a thin quarto between two voluminous dictionaries on a bookseller's shelf" (*FF,* I, 180). And then, of course, there is Melford's well-known contrast between Humphry and Dutton which has it that "Humphry may be compared to an English pudding, composed of good wholesome flour and suet, and Dutton to a syllabub or iced froth, which, though agreeable to the taste, has nothing solid or substantial" (*HC,* II, 40). It would be no difficult task to compile from Smollett's imagery an index to the range of his interests: the sea, medicine, natural science, the arts, classical antiquity—all his main preoccupations are at various times reflected in the figurative language he uses. Never, it is true, are the figures as elaborate or as artfully wrought as are, for instance, Fielding's Homeric similes: characteristically, they seem to be struck off rapidly, casual and unpremeditated, the inspiration of a moment rather than the product of deliberate planning, and it is for this reason, of course, that their quality is so uneven. And yet, perhaps just because of this very spontaneity, they are diverse and complex enough to merit a separate study.

3

But this is not the place for it; and we must now turn to the middle section of our paragraph and, specifically, to the matter of its diction. Framed by two exclamations, Don Diego's solemn tribute to Providence and Joshua's slightly comical Biblical analogy, these short sentences, it will be recalled, list the reactions of the bystanders. One notices that they do so in an orderly manner, that is to say, in an order of descending importance of the characters, with the central figures, Monimia and Renaldo, coming first, followed by Madam Clement, Monimia's protectress and stepmother-to-be, and the clergyman and the doctor, minor characters indeed, bringing up the rear. But, before we go on, it might be well to reproduce the passage once more: "So saying," it reads, "he fell upon her neck, and wept aloud. The tears of sympathetic joy trickled down her snowy bosom, that heaved with rapture inexpressible. Renaldo's eyes poured forth the briny stream. The cheeks of Madam Clement were not dry in this conjuncture; she kneeled by Serafina, kissed her with all the eagerness of maternal affection, and with uplifted hands adored the Power that preordained this blessed event. The clergyman and doctor intimately shared the general transport."

Smollett's point, of course, is simply that the affecting scene they have just witnessed has moved all present to tears. But he cannot dramatize this effect without listing each character's reaction in turn; and once having committed himself to this method, he apparently thinks he has to avoid repeating the same phraseology. He solves this problem by resorting to what has come to be known as "elegant variation." While the Don—in all plainness—is said to be weeping, Monimia, we find, has tears of sympathetic joy trickling down her snowy bosom, Renaldo's eyes pour forth the briny stream, Madam Clement's cheeks are not dry, the clergyman and doctor share the general transport, and Joshua has tears of true benevolence flowing from his eyes: their emotions, one might almost say, are proportionate to their importance in the story—with Monimia's and Renaldo's expressed in positive terms, Madam Clement's in negative and the clergyman's and doctor's in general ones. Only Joshua breaks this pattern.

The language is obviously stylized and highly conventional: a bosom is "snowy," rapture is "inexpressible," an event is "blessed." It makes lavish use of commonplace eighteenth-century periphrasis: eyes pour forth "the briny stream," "drops of true benevolence" flow from eyes, voices resemble the hoarse notes of "the long-eared tribe." It "dallies with Latininity":[8] this "conjuncture," "maternal affection," "preordained." And most striking of all perhaps, it reinforces the artificiality of those devices by, in a sense, depersonalizing the emotions it describes: it is not so much the individuals who choose to shed tears or decide against keeping their cheeks dry as the tears which, having achieved a sort of autonomy, decide to trickle down snowy bosoms, and the cheeks which refrain from staying dry. The effect of all this, I suppose, is to generalize the emotions. We are reminded that, after all, it is not a particular girl, Monimia, or a particular lad, Renaldo, who has been deeply moved, but the heroine and the hero. Utimately, in short, the emotion counts for more than the person who happens to be experiencing it; and this might explain why the "formulas," in which hair bristled, teeth chattered and knees knocked, took the syntactical form they did.

Smollett's prose style has often been extravagantly praised. V. S. Pritchett has called it a "sane, impartial style,"[9] Herbert Read a "clean impersonal mode, devoid of mannerisms,"[10] and Alan D. McKillop a "brilliant, graphic, and varied style."[11] Doubtless all these commendations can be substantiated by

[8] The phrase is Sir Arthur Quiller-Couch's. See his *On the Art of Writing* (Cambridge, England, 1921), p. 84.

[9] *Books in General* (London, 1953), p. 89.

[10] *Collected Essays in Literary Criticism* (London, 1938), p. 237.

[11] *Early Masters*, p. 152.

reference to certain parts of Smollett; and yet, one cannot help wondering whether in making their judgments as broad as they have, the critics allowed for all those parts of Smollett which, like the passage we have just inspected, simply do not fit their description. In the light of what we have found, one is more likely to agree with James Sutherland's charge that "as early as *Roderick Random* . . . Smollett shows a fondness for pompous diction that certainly borders on the pedantic." [12] Here, for example, is a representative sentence from the very beginning of *Roderick Random* which, it seems to me, fully bears out Professor Sutherland's allegation: "My father being informed of what had happened, flew to the embraces of his darling spouse, and, while he loaded his offspring with paternal caresses, could not forbear shedding a flood of tears, on beholding the dear partner of his heart, for whose ease he would have sacrificed the treasures of the East, stretched upon a flock bed in a miserable apartment, unable to protect her from the inclemencies of the weather" (*RR*, I, 4–5).

In passages such as this—as much as in our paragraph—the self-conscious attempt at an elevated style has betrayed Smollett into the use of trite eighteenth-century diction and hackneyed periphrasis—with a result that is little more than a skillful pastiche of ready-made phrases. Now, it must be granted, of course, that Smollett is perfectly capable of turning the same sort of language to excellent advantage when he uses it ironically —as witness the following: "When he had paid the reckoning, we sallied out, roaring and singing; and were conducted by our

---

[12] "Some Aspects of Eighteenth-Century Prose," *Essays on the Eighteenth Century* (Oxford, 1945), p. 108.

leader to a place of nocturnal entertainment, where I immediately attached myself to a fair one, with whom I proposed to spend the remaining part of the night; but she not relishing my appearance, refused to grant my request before I had made her an acknowledgment; which not suiting my circumstances, we broke off our correspondence, to my no small mortification and resentment, because I thought the mercenary creature had not done justice to my merit" (*RR,* I, 121). Some of the very best things in Smollett, one remembers, work in just this way. We should bear in mind too that it is precisely the stylization of his phraseology which helps to create that formality and artificiality which Smollett, accepting the conventions of his time, tends to strive for in his accounts of high life. And finally, of course, it ought not to be forgotten that Smollett modified this style over the years. As Louis L. Martz has convincingly shown, the many years of hack work produced a remarkable change—"from elaboration to simplicity, from expansiveness to succinctness, from turgidity to precision"[13]—so that the later works are comparatively free of the qualities we have been noticing. Nevertheless, the fact remains that it will surely be necessary to allow for the cliché-ridden diction of our passage in any comprehensive attempt to characterize Smollett's style.

4

I need hardly say that in the foregoing I have not pretended to undertake such an attempt. Indeed, as I look back over what I have said, I am dismayed to find how little my glosses on one paragraph have done to account for the robustness and verve of

[13] *The Later Career of Tobias Smollett* (New Haven, 1942), p. 16.

style which most readers of Smollett will rightly consider to be peculiarly his. If anything, in fact, I may be thought to have dwelled at undue length on the limitations of his manner— on the stylistic handicaps he labored under when trying for pathos and on the staleness of his diction. And yet, I think, I could fairly be maintained that Smollett's weaknesses—at least in part—explain his strengths, and that inferences as to his manner may as successfully be drawn from a passage that does not represent him at his best as from one that does.

This much, at any rate, is clear. There is no such thing as one kind of Smollett: Smollett dealing with high life differs from Smollett dealing with low life, Smollett describing differs from Smollett narrating, Smollett satirizing differs from Smollett moralizing, Smollett treating romantic love differs from Smollett treating animal lust; the man, in short, who wrote "The tears of sympathetic joy trickled down her snowy bosom, that heaved with rapture inexpressible," is a very different kind of writer from the one who could say "while he skipped about the room in an awkward ecstasy"; different in tone, different in diction, and different even in syntax. This is all the more true since, as Professor McKillop has pointed out, there is lacking in Smollett—not always, but generally—what is usually present in Fielding, the *persona* of the detached narrator who takes a playful attitude toward his own rhetoric and that of his characters.[14] In the absence of such ironic qualification to serve as a kind of common denominator, it is no easy matter to isolate the authentic "voice" of Tobias Smollett.

Certainly, no single paragraph will do it. But such a para-

[14] *Early Masters*, p. 152.

graph may at least yield us some useful pointers. The passage we have been working with does, I think, exactly that. Above all else, it demonstrates the essentially pictorial and dramatic quality of Smollett's art. "A novel," Smollett wrote in a now famous preface to *Ferdinand Count Fathom,* "is a large diffused picture, comprehending the characters of life, disposed in different groups, and exhibited in various attitudes, for the purposes of an uniform plan, and general occurrence, to which every individual figure is subservient." And he continued: "But this plan cannot be executed with propriety, probability, or success, without a principal personage to attract the attention, unite the incidents, unwind the clue of the labyrinth, and at last close the scene, by virtue of his own importance" (*FF,* I, 3). Professor McKillop has reminded us that in Smollett's time the word "group" is still largely a painter's term, and that, in fact, painting and the drama supply the analogies underlying this definition.[15] How closely these two media were associated in Smollett's mind with what he was doing is, I think, reflected in our paragraph. As they are arranged in it, the figures clearly constitute a sort of dramatic tableau, "comprehending the characters of life, disposed in different groups, and exhibited in various attitudes"; and indeed, it would not be too much to say that the same holds of some of the most memorable episodes in Smollett: Roderick's first visit to the ordinary, let us say, and the Feast in the Manner of the Ancients. In each of these cases, moreover, the scene receives a special piquancy from the great diversity of individuals present. It might thus be relevant to notice that in our paragraph no less than five nationalities are

[15] *Early Masters,* pp. 164–65.

represented: the Don and his daughter are Spaniards, Renaldo is a Hungarian, Madam Clement a Frenchwoman, the clergyman and doctor Englishmen, and Joshua a Jew—"the characters of life" in more ways than one.

The dramatic tableau method used here, to repeat a point already made, exacts a heavy price. By rigidly restricting a writer to the external manifestations of the inner life, it denies him the possibility of recording finer nuances of feeling—with consequences that are evident in the opening sentence of our paragraph. Here, in the attempt to suggest the Don's complex state of mind, Smollett is forced to fall back upon items from a readily available repertoire of set phrases devised to describe intense emotion. But what works to the disadvantage of an attempt at pathos contributes to the achievement of comedy: physical reflexes may be unsatisfactory as indices to human emotions, but when heightened to grotesque proportions they become very funny indeed. In short, we are far more likely to be amused at Joshua "skipping about the room in an awkward ecstasy" than we are likely to be touched by the tears of the others.

Our paragraph thus suggest why Smollett fails so wretchedly with pathos, why he lacks resources to deal with romantic love, why, in fact, he is ill-equipped to cope with anything that affects the human heart. But on the positive side, it also helps to explain why he succeeds so brilliantly with farcical comedy. A kind of microcosm of the entire novel, it thus mirrors Smollett's excellencies as well as his limitations. And indeed, it does a great deal more. By reminding us of the pictorial as well as the dramatic qualities of Smollett's art, it brings home to us what

might be called its impersonality, its intellectuality. In a pene-
trating introduction to *Joseph Andrews,* Maynard Mack speaks
of the comic artist who, he says, "subordinates the presentation
of life as experience, where the relationship between ourselves
and the characters experiencing it is a primary one, to the
presentation of life as spectacle, where the primary relationship
is between himself and us as onlookers." [16] Just such a "presentation of life as spectacle" is the essence of Smollett's manner.
For all that he lacks Fielding's ironic detachment, he too, though
in a different way, is never anything but the onlooker who
remains outside the characters he portrays. The very language
he uses, a language which, as we saw, divorces emotions from
the persons experiencing them and attributes to them a kind
of autonomous existence, reinforces the separation. And, of
course, it is only by virtue of being an observer that Smollett
can recognize and exult in displaying his fellow creatures'
affinity with the animal kingdom.

Such a stance comes naturally to Tobias Smollett, the "beg-
garly Scot" who, for all the mortifications he suffered from
what he took to be "the selfishness, envy, malice, and base indifference of mankind" (*RR,* I, xlii), eventually made good
in the rough-and-tumble world of Grub Street. His was an
orderly, but neither a reflective nor an analytical mind. What
it lacked in profundity, however, it made up for in boundless
energy. The misanthropic, world-weary pose the doctor sometimes fancied is surely deceptive. It covers up an insatiable
curiosity about people and things, not, to be sure, the searching
curiosity of the self-examined thinker, but rather the darting

[16] In the Rinehart ed. (New York, 1948), p. xv.

inquisitiveness of the scientifically-oriented medical man who keeps a wary eye on what goes on around him. He is not so much the traveler, I should say then, as he is the alert tourist, a man impelled to travel, literally as well as literarily, by an irrepressible hankering to be "in the know." Hence the crowdedness of his canvas, hence the profusion of people, places and incidents in his novels—and hence also the multiplicity and diversity of his styles. If his impatient restlessness prevents him from sustaining for long any one mood or any one style, it is also the source of his immense gusto and vitality. And it may well be that *Humphry Clinker* is his finest work because the epistolary method as he here has molded it to his use legitimized a variety of styles and moods that was more congenial to his restless temperament than anything he had ever tried before.

S. F. Johnson

Hardy and Burke's "Sublime"

In the course of his quarrel with the drama of modern manners, Yeats argued that the worst plays are those about "modern educated people," since their language "cannot become impassioned . . . without making somebody gushing and sentimental. Educated and well-bred people . . . have no powerful language at all." He found, however, that

> Ibsen understood the difficulty and made all his characters a little provincial . . . and made a leading article sort of poetry . . . it was possible to believe them using in their moments of excitement, and if the play needed more than that, they could always do something stupid.[1]

Like Ibsen, Thomas Hardy was a largely self-educated provincial, uncomfortable with modern manners and awkward with the language of educated and well-bred people. In his "novels" he employed techniques much like those that Yeats found in Ibsen, except that Hardy, whose characters are relatively static under changing events, met the demands of serial publication by making his universe, rather than his characters, do something stupid.

Most of Hardy's critics have commented on his awkward style and geometric construction, both in prose and verse. In

[1] *The Cutting of an Agate* (New York, 1912), pp. 73–74.

the latter R. P. Blackmur sees the work of a formula-ridden mind, "a naturally primitive intelligence, schematized beyond discrimination." [2] In the former Frank Chapman finds "a clumsy aiming at impressiveness," although he concludes that "this clumsy, polysyllabic style is not ordinary journalese, but stands for real character." [3] The character it stands for is, of course, that of Hardy himself, who so often intrudes between the reader and the fiction.

Hardy's own comments on style cannot be taken at face value. Most of them echo a note he made in 1875: "The whole secret of a living style and the difference between it and a dead style, lies in not having too much style—being, in fact, a little careless, or rather seeming to be, here and there." [4] In his later years, he said much the same thing about poetic style when he remarked that he never wrote more than three or four drafts of a poem for fear of spoiling its freshness.[5]

Hardy's practise reveals that he must have thought of style as ornamental, inorganic, even mechanical, as something separate from and subordinate to the ideas expressed or the action or scene described. A late poem, "Whispered at the Church-opening," makes this clear in its contrast between the "eloquent" and successful bishop and the unsuccessful vicar, "sincerest of all; / Whose words, though unpicked, gave the essence of things." Like his vicar, Hardy is always sincere, often painfully so; but his words are rarely "unpicked." He felt that language was

[2] *Language as Gesture* (New York, 1952), p. 74.

[3] "Hardy the Novelist," *Scrutiny,* III (1935), pp. 26, 36.

[4] Florence Emily Hardy, *The Early Life of Thomas Hardy: 1840–1891* (New York, 1928), p. 138.

[5] Robert Graves, *Good-bye to All That* (New York, 1957), p. 305.

clothing for wordless conceptions, and although his own remarks would lead us to expect simplicity of style, "Robes loosely flowing," what we get are "all th' adulteries of art"—whether in his prose, with its set pieces of description and philosophical rumination, or in much of his verse, forced as it is into arbitrary and elaborate stanzaic shapes and metrical molds. However important *what* he said was to him, it is obvious that he labored over *how* to say it.

In the earlier 1870s, at least, Hardy was an architect in search of a literary style. In 1873 and 1874, during the composition and serial publication of *Far from the Madding Crowd,* Hardy turned frequently to his editor, Leslie Stephen, for criticism and advice, apparently even for reading lists. Stephen once wrote him: "I think as a critic, that the less authors read of criticism the better. You, e.g., have a perfectly fresh and original vein, and I think the less you bother yourself about critical canons the less chance there is of your becoming self-conscious and cramped." [6]

Hardy seems not to have heeded this advice. As Morton Zabel writes,

> his methodical habit of mind exercised itself over many years in notations on structure, form, style, and aesthetic ideas, and in a continuous effort to generalize these into working principles. . . . His scruples as a workman and his methodical seriousness as a student, even his systematic ambition for literary fame, were outbalanced by his sense of being an outsider to art's higher mysteries. [7]

[6] *Early Life of Thomas Hardy,* p. 143; the letter is dated May 16, 1876.
[7] *Craft and Character* (New York, 1957), pp. 73, 77.

As a young man, Hardy had mastered the crafts of architecture, and he seems to have determined to master literary craftsmanship in much the same way—that is, by serving an apprenticeship and studying the theory and notable examples of the practise of the art. His note on style, from which I have already quoted, begins: "Read again Addison, Macaulay, Newman, Sterne, Defoe, Lamb, Gibbon, Burke, Times Leaders, etc., in a study of style." None of these masters seems to have influenced his style directly, excepting perhaps Times Leaders. Of the others, Burke is most important; although he influenced Hardy's style only indirectly, he seems to have influenced Hardy's conception of literary effectiveness significantly.

Whatever other of Burke's *Works* he may have tasted, Hardy chewed and digested *A Philosophical Enquiry into the Origin of our Ideas of the Sublime and Beautiful.* In *Far from the Madding Crowd* he paraphrases Burke's unusual definition of "delight," [8] but he seems to have read the *Enquiry* too late for it to have had any particular influence on the conception of that book. It had a more definite effect on both the conception and execution of his next major work, *The Return of the Native*.

I have elsewhere pointed out that Hardy borrowed both information and phraseology from a passage in the *Enquiry* in order to construct a thematically significant paragraph about Mrs. Yeobright's intuition:

[8] Carl J. Weber, *Hardy and the Lady from Madison Square* (Waterville, Maine, 1952), p. 89. I wish to thank Professor Weber, the dean of American Hardy scholars, and Professors Lawrance Thompson, Walter E. Houghton, Geoffrey Tillotson, William Elton, David Cowden, and Howard H. Schless for help and encouragement over many years in the developing of this material.

She had a singular insight into life, considering that she had never mixed with it. There are instances of persons who, without clear ideas of the things they criticize, have yet had clear ideas of the relations of those things. Blacklock, a poet blind from his birth, could describe visual objects with accuracy; Professor Sanderson, who was also blind, gave excellent lectures on colour, and taught others the theory of ideas which they had and he had not.[9]   (p. 223)

Burke's original statement is part of his controversial attempt to demonstrate that "WORDS may affect without raising IMAGES":

Since I wrote these papers I found two very striking instances of the possibility there is, that a man may hear words without having any idea of the things which they represent, and yet afterwards be capable of returning them to others, combined in a new way. . . . The first instance, is that of Mr. Blacklock, a poet blind from his birth. Few men blessed with the most perfect sight can describe visual objects with more spirit and justness than this blind man; which cannot possibly be attributed to his having a clearer conception of the things he describes than is common to other persons. . . . The second instance is of Mr.

---

[9] All references to *The Return of the Native* in this essay are to the Library Edition (London, 1949); they are given in parentheses following each quotation. The Library Edition is identical in text and pagination with the Wessex and Anniversary editions; I have not used the more widely owned Modern Library edition because its text is not the final one approved by Hardy.

I called attention to Hardy's borrowing in the *Times Literary Supplement,* Dec. 7, 1956, p. 731, and privately communicated to the editor much of the material that appears on p. cxviii of J. T. Boulton's edition of Burke's *Enquiry* (London and New York, 1958).

Saunderson, professor of mathematics in the university
of Cambridge . . . he gave excellent lectures upon light
and colours; and this man taught others the theory of
those ideas which they had, and which he himself undoubtedly had not.[10]   (V, v)

This passage occurs near the end of the *Enquiry,* where
Burke sets forth his theory of *how* words affect us in literature.
Hardy must have felt, in reading this book, that he was indeed
learning something of the secrets of literary craftsmanship,
particularly since Burke prefaces his analyses of the causes of
the sublime and beautiful with the comment that "a consideration of the rationale of our passions seems to me very necessary
for all who would affect them upon solid and sure principles"
(I, xix). Burke concludes the *Enquiry* as follows:

It was not my design to enter into the criticism of the
sublime and beautiful in any art, but to attempt to lay
down such principles as may tend to ascertain, to distinguish, and to form a sort of standard for them; which
purposes I thought might be best effected by an enquiry
into the properties of such things in nature as raise love
and astonishment in us; and by shewing in what manner
they operated to produce these passions. Words were only
so far to be considered, as to shew upon what principle
they were capable of being the representatives of these
natural things, and by what powers they were able to

[10] *A Philosophical Enquiry* . . . , ed. by J. T. Boulton (London and New
York, 1958), p. 169. All references to the *Enquiry* in this essay are to this edition, but since earlier reprints are more widely distributed I cite by part and
section numbers in parentheses following each quotation.

affect us often as strongly as the things they represent, and sometimes much more strongly. (V, vii)

I think it can be demonstrated that Hardy used the *Enquiry* as a handbook for "sublime" effects when he wrote *The Return of the Native;* but the demonstration is tedious.[11] Therefore I shall simply assume some such relationship. I do not, of course, mean to imply that Hardy took all the ideas, images, and effects for which there are parallels in the *Enquiry* from Burke; he was quite as aware as Burke, or anyone else, of those objects in nature that "raise love and astonishment in us," and he was thoroughly familiar with the "sublime" in literature, particularly in the works of two of his favorite poets, Byron and Shelley.[12] I am not claiming that Burke's *Enquiry* was in

[11] Such a demonstration would involve comparison of similar passages in *Far from the Madding Crowd* and *The Return of the Native;* for example, the beginning of the second chapter of the former and much of the first chapter of the latter, the descriptions of fires in both (chap. 6 and Book I, chap. 3, respectively), the philosophical ruminations on the Shearing barn (chap. 22) and passages on Rainbarrow and the traditionalism of the peasants (p. 459), the description of the storm in chapter 37 of *Far from the Madding Crowd* and similar descriptions in *Return of the Native* (see below). It would also involve an examination of Hardy's intervening book, *The Hand of Ethelberta*, which Leslie Stephen edited.

[12] As my colleague Marjorie Hope Nicolson has pointed out to me, Hardy may have read Addison's "The Pleasures of the Imagination" (*Spectator*, Nos. 411–421), a major source for Burke's *Enquiry*, in his "study of style" in 1875. She has also pointed out that Addison and Byron are particularly impressed by "greatness" ("sublimity") in architecture as well as in nature. Hardy himself singled out Byron and Shelley as the authors of his favorite poems in *The Fortnightly Review*, August, 1887, along with passages from Carlyle and the Book of Samuel as his favorite prose. For discussion of Shelley as one of Hardy's favorite poets, see the articles by Phyllis Bartlett: "Hardy's Shelley," *Keats-Shelley Journal*, IV (1955), 15–29, and "Seraph of Heaven: A Shelleyan Dream in Hardy's Fiction," *PMLA*, LXX (1955), 624–35.

any sense an important "source" for Hardy; rather it was an "influence." Hardy's reading of the *Enquiry* not only may have given him some new ideas, it must also have heightened his awareness of some causes of the "sublime" and have reinforced a number of his own preconceptions and predilections as a writer.

Although Hardy uses a variety of styles, including a straightforward one for narrating action and at least two very different ones for dialogue, I shall focus primarily on the "clumsy, polysyllabic style" he affects in those descriptions and philosophical ruminations that aim most directly at "sublimity." [13] Hardy's critics agree that those passages are ponderous, pretentious, and overwritten, and that nonetheless they manage to create powerful and memorable effects. Even so unsympathetic a critic as T. S. Eliot allows Hardy some high marks: "He was indifferent even to the prescripts of good writing; he wrote sometimes overpoweringly well, but always very carelessly; at times his style touches sublimity without ever having passed through the stage of being good." [14] One of

---

[13] The categories of Burke's "sublime" are most frequent in such passages. The greatest density of Burke's categories in *The Return of the Native* occurs in Books I, V ("The Discovery"), and III ("The Fascination"); Book II ("The Arrival") is least dense in this respect, and the very short Book VI ("Aftercourses") is rather more dense than Book IV. Maximum density occurs in the opening descriptions of the heath and of Eustacia and again at the catastrophe.

[14] *After Strange Gods* (New York, 1934), p. 59. Mr. Eliot's penchant for epigrammatically memorable statements reminds me of the Johnsonian counterpart to this one: "An essential point to make about Seneca is the consistency of his writing, its maintenance on one level, below which he seldom falls and above which he never mounts." *Selected Essays, 1917–1932* (New York, 1932), p. 60.

our own best stylists, Katherine Anne Porter, is far more sympathetic:

> Hardy was not a careless writer. . . . He wrote and wrote again, and he never found it easy. . . . His prose lumbers along, it jogs, it creaks, it hesitates. . . . That celebrated first scene on Egdon Heath. . . . Who does not remember it? And in actual rereading, what could be duller? What could be more labored than his introduction of the widow Yeobright at the heath fire among the dancers, or more unconvincing than the fears of the timid boy that the assembly are literally raising the Devil? Except for this; in my memory of that episode, as in dozens of others in many of Hardy's novels, I have seen it, I was there. When I read it, it almost disappears from view, and afterward comes back, phraseless, living in its somber clearness, as Hardy meant it to do, I feel certain. This to my view is the chief quality of good prose as distinguished from poetry. By his own testimony, he limited his territory by choice. . . . In the end his work was the sum of his experience, he arrived at his particular true testimony; along the way, sometimes, many times, he wrote sublimely.[15]

This is the best that has been said for Hardy's prose style, and it is perhaps all we need to know about it when we are talking of style as immediate surface texture alone.[16] But style is, as

---

[15] *The Days Before* (New York, 1952), p. 35.

[16] Other remarkable discussions of Hardy's prose style are those by Vernon Lee, in her brilliant book *The Handling of Words* (London, 1923), pp. 222–41; John Holloway in *The Victorian Sage* (London, 1953), pp. 244–89; and (*echt Deutsch*) the dissertation of Peter Aliesch, *Studien zu Thomas Hardy's Prosastil* (Berne, 1941).

Miss Porter implies, far more than that, and we can, I think, examine Hardy's style for the means by which it sometimes touches the "sublimity" that Mr. Eliot, Miss Porter, and many others have found in it. One way of doing so is to use Burke's *Enquiry* as a guidebook, much as Hardy seems to have used it as a handbook.

Part Two of the *Enquiry* deals directly with the sources of the SUBLIME, "the strongest emotion which the mind is capable of feeling" (I, VII). Its twenty-two sections treat of those elements in nature and architecture (II, x, xv) which produce such emotion in man. These are chiefly, to use Burke's own headings, TERROR, OBSCURITY, POWER (particularly the idea of great power as· of God or fate), PRIVATION (or solitude), VASTNESS and INFINITY, DIFFICULTY (Burke's example is Stonehenge), MAGNIFICENCE, LIGHT and COLOR, certain sounds, smells, and tastes, and FEELING (especially bodily pain). Hardy, of course, intermingles a large number of these categories, in accordance perhaps with Burke's precept that "a great profusion of things which are splendid or valuable in themselves, is *magnificent*":

> There are . . . many descriptions in the poets and orators which owe their sublimity to a richness and profusion of images, in which the mind is so dazzled as to make it impossible to attend to that exact coherence and agreement of the allusions, which we should require on every other occasion.   (II, XIII)
> The mind is hurried out of itself, by a croud of great and confused images; which affect because they are crouded

and confused. For separate them, and you lose much of the greatness, and join them, and you infallibly lose the clearness. (II, IV)

For the sake of such "clearness," I have undertaken to separate Hardy's "profusion of images" into their Burkean categories.

In discussing the first of his categories, TERROR, Burke asserts that whatever is terrible with regard to sight is sublime whether it be "endued with greatness of dimensions or not. . . . As serpents and poisonous animals of almost all kinds" (II, II). Hardy's use of an adder to effect the turning point of his plot, the death of Mrs. Yeobright, climaxes half a dozen widely scattered references to snakes, scorpions, and stinging insects.[17] Burke continues:

And to things of great dimensions, if we annex an adventitious idea of terror, they become without comparison greater. A level plain of a vast extent on land, is certainly no mean idea; the prospect of such a plain may be as extensive as a prospect of the ocean; but can it ever fill the mind with any thing so great as the ocean itself? (II, II)

Hardy undertakes to answer Burke's question in his opening description of Egdon Heath:

The great inviolate place had an ancient permanence which the sea cannot claim. Who can say of a particular sea that it is old? Distilled by the sun, kneaded by the moon, it is renewed in a year, in a day, or in an hour. The sea changed, the fields changed, the rivers, the villages, and the people changed, yet Egdon remained. (p. 7)

[17] Pages 349–50; compare pp. 79, 205, 298, 326, 433.

Hardy's heath is, however, modified from the idea of a vast level plain in accordance with Burke's precept that "the effects of a rugged and broken surface seem stronger than where it is smooth and polished" (II, VII); it is a "heathy, furzy, briary wilderness" (p. 6) whose surfaces "were neither so steep as to be destructible by weather, nor so flat as to be the victims of floods and deposits" (p. 7). At one point, Hardy for obvious reasons does make the heath level. It is where Clym has decided to marry Eustacia despite his mother's objections. The time is sunset, in the late spring:

> the dead flat of the scenery overpowered him. . . . There was something in its oppressive horizontality which . . . gave him a sense of bare equality with, and no superiority to, a single living thing under the sun.   (p. 245)

Hardy recurrently contrasts the vastness of his scene with the insignificance of man, and the scene's permanence, its resistance to destruction, with the disastrous chances that afflict his characters. Such recurrence is structural, that is, stylistic in a larger sense than that which we apply to the dissection of isolated sentences and paragraphs. Those phrases and sentences that I have just quoted from Hardy exhibit the characteristics we are accustomed to find in the "impressive" meditative and descriptive style. It depends heavily on nouns and adjectives; where it is not entirely passive, it proceeds slowly, by accumulation; like much poetry, it operates non-logically, even counterlogically, by association. Hardy's "style" is rarely effective locally; rather it *becomes* effective when accumulated associations are reawakened at appropriate turning points in his narrative.

Burke's second category, OBSCURITY, that is, darkness and gloom, is of primary importance in *The Return of the Native*. The main action, omitting the final section, "Aftercourses," in accordance with Hardy's own suggestion,[18] is framed by two November nights which contrast sharply with the garish, stifling August day chosen for Mrs. Yeobright's death. The heath is a "near relation of night" and when night comes "the obscurity in the air and the obscurity in the land closed together in a black fraternization towards which each advanced half-way" (p. 4). It attains intensity

> during winter darkness, tempests, and mists . . . for the storm was its lover, and the wind its friend. Then it became the home of strange phantoms; and it was found to be the hitherto unrecognized original of those wild regions of obscurity which are vaguely felt to be compassing us about in midnight dreams of flight and disaster.
>
> (pp. 5–6; cf. pp. 3, 420–21)

Eustacia is the "Queen of Night," with hair so dark that "to see [it] was to fancy that a whole winter did not contain enough darkness to form its shadow: it closed over her forehead like nightfall extinguishing the western glow" (p. 75). Her eyes are dark and wild—even the peasants remark on this fact (p. 56)—and "full of nocturnal mysteries" (p. 76). She is given over to "sudden fits of gloom, one of the phases of the night-side of sentiment which she knew too well for her years," and her presence brings memories of, among other things, "tropical midnights" (p. 76).

It is perhaps unjust to isolate inappropriate similes that are

---

[18] See Hardy's note to Book VI, chap. 3, p. 473.

barely functional to Hardy's patterns of recurrent association, but they are part of Hardy's "style." Two examples, in the category DARKNESS are a description of Eustacia and Wildeve walking on the moonlit heath—"To an eye above them their two faces would have appeared amid the expanse like two pearls on a table of ebony" (p. 313)—and the more grotesque description of Charley appearing "on the dark ridge of heathland, like a fly on a negro" (p. 149).

Burke's next major category is POWER, specifically the power to inflict pain and death. The extreme instance is God Himself:

> Some reflection, some comparing is necessary to satisfy us of his wisdom, his justice, and his goodness; to be struck with his power, it is only necessary that we should open our eyes. But whilst we contemplate so vast an object . . . we shrink into the minuteness of our own nature, and are, in a manner, annihilated before him.   (II, v)

Hardy's use of POWER is central to his work, whether it be in the interrelations of his characters—who is in whose power and when [19]—or, more significantly, in the relations between his characters and the "coquettish . . . Providence" (p. 140) of their universe, conceived, to be sure, in terms that would have shocked Burke.[20]

Eustacia is the most powerful of the characters. The peasants

[19] Compare the suggestive but over-ingenious analysis of the action of *The Return of the Native* as "a mechanical concatenation of seven hour-glass plots" by R. W. Stallman, "Hardy's Hour-glass Novel," *Sewanee Review*, LV (1947), 283–96.

[20] The word "power" is used nearly twenty times in the book, and there are many uses of synonymous terms as well (for example, pp. 49, 72, 73, 77, 96, 103, 104, 108, 154, 161, 184, 187, 265, 284, 303).

think she is a witch, and the sense of her mysterious power is heightened by Hardy's references to her as queenly, or even divine. The "Queen of Night" chapter is a set piece of character description that balances the earlier set piece on Egdon Heath. They are the two thick pillars of rhetoric on which Hardy supports his structure, and they create major expectations about the relationship between the protagonist and the scene—indeed they define the action as a conflict between the power of Eustacia and the power of the heath.

The "Queen of Night" chapter begins:

> Eustacia Vye was the raw material of a divinity. . . . She had the passions and instincts that make a model goddess, that is, those which make not quite a model woman. Had it been possible for the earth and mankind to be entirely in her grasp for a while . . . few in the world would have noticed the change of government. There would have been the same inequality of lot, the same heaping up of favours here, of contumely there, the same generosity before justice, the same perpetual dilemmas, the same captious alteration of caresses and blows that we endure now.   (p. 75)

The style here has the characteristics I have pointed out in passages describing the heath. In both chapters Hardy is, among other things, presenting raw materials which will take significant shape as recurrent associations begin to accumulate. An important one here is the "inequality of lot" associated with Eustacia. Just before her suicide she exclaims "I do not deserve my lot!" (p. 422), and earlier Hardy tells us that she shifted blame from herself to "some indistinct, colossal Prince of the World, who had framed her situation and ruled her lot"(p. 353).

The idea is even incorporated in Hardy's choice, surely "epistemic," of her surname, since "vye" once had the meaning "way of, or lot in, life" (*O. E. D. sb.*[1] 2).

Hardy's major emphasis is not so much on the power of his characters as on the power of nature and supernature, associated with the heath. The narrative is less concerned with characters in conflict than with a demonstration of the ironic effects on them of powers outside their control. The heath does not serve, as one critic would have it, "merely as a magnificent backdrop" for an action to which "any other environment would, essentially, be equally congruous."[21] Rather, as D. H. Lawrence recognized,[22] the action stems directly from the effects of the heath on the central characters, a fact that is stressed by Eustacia's criss-crossing the heath in her correlative changes of lot and habitation. To her the heath is a jail (pp. 106, 413; cf. p. 4) out of which she tries and fails to break, and the waters of Shadwater Weir are its final, impassable boundary.

The power of nature is exemplified by storms, culminating in the storm on the night of the catastrophe. Here Hardy directly imitates *King Lear* (see his 1895 preface) and baldly states, as he frequently does, the effect he is aiming at: "Never was harmony more perfect than that between the chaos of her [Eustacia's] mind and the chaos of the world without" (p. 421). More implicitly, Hardy contrasts the destruction of Eustacia with the indestructibility of the heath in a series of images of storm that anticipate the catastrophe, notably in the storm on

[21] Carl H. Grabo, *The Technique of the Novel* (New York, 1928), pp. 132, 139.

[22] "Six Novels of Thomas Hardy and the Real Tragedy," *The Book-Collector's Quarterly*, V (1932), 44–61.

the June day Clym chooses to find a house for himself and Eustacia. The trees on the edge of the heath are "undergoing amputations, bruises, cripplings, and harsh lacerations. . . . Yet a few yards to Yeobright's left, on the open heath, how ineffectively gnashed the storm! . . . Egdon was made for such times as these" (p. 247; cf. p. 329).

Supernatural power is treated at levels ranging from witches and ghosts to "Heaven" and fate. I shall discuss these "images" briefly at more appropriate places later in this essay.

Burke's next category, PRIVATION, is used by Hardy chiefly as solitude. The heath has a lonely face; "solitude seemed to look out of its countenance" (p. 6). Like its mysterious agent, Diggory Venn, it is "Ishmaelitish" (pp. 6, 175). Rainbarrow, the huge Celtic burial mound "occupied the loftiest ground of the loneliest height that the heath contained. . . . It formed the pole and axis of this heathery world" (p. 13). It is, in fact, contrasted with Paris, "the centre and vortex of the fashionable world" (p. 128) which Clym rejects and Eustacia desires.

Eustacia's loneliness is often mentioned (pp. 56, 78–80, 101, 173, 416, 421). Her grandfather's house is "the loneliest of lonely houses on these thinly populated slopes" (p. 83; cf. pp. 67, 114); it is the house nearest the center of the heath. Wildeve complains of the loneliness of the heath and suggests that Eustacia escape with him to Wisconsin (p. 98). Venn, who remains aloof from other itinerants, has an occupation that tends to isolate him, "and isolated he was mostly seen to be" (p. 90). Mrs. Yeobright has "something of an estranged mien: the solitude exhaled from the heath was concentrated in this face that had risen from it" (p. 35; cf. pp. 241, 255). Even

Thomasin, Eustacia's foil, is at one point seen as "solitary and undefended except by the power of her own hope" (p. 187). It is Clym who is finally loneliest of all. His "look suggested isolation" (p. 162). He plans to live with Eustacia "in absolute seclusion" (p. 244; cf. pp. 283–84) and rents a house "almost as lonely as that of Eustacia's grandfather" (p. 247). Hardy stresses his utter isolation after the catastrophe (pp. 426, 455, 483).

Burke's next category is VASTNESS, which includes "the last extreme of littleness" as well as "greatness of dimension" (II, VII), one of several instances "wherein the opposite extremes operate equally in favour of the sublime" (II, XIV).[23] Vastness is, of course, the keynote of the opening of the book and, as we have already seen, recurrent in it. The microscopic perspective also occurs and recurs—for example, in the descriptions of minute worlds of insects and other small animals as seen by Mrs. Yeobright in her fatal journey across the heath: "occasion-ally she came to a spot where independent worlds of ephemerons were passing their time in mad carousal" (p. 327; cf. pp. 225, 330, 342–43). That these worlds stand in metaphoric relation to the world of men on the heath is clear in a passage describing Clym's assimilation to it when, because of his near-blindness, he has become a furze-cutter:

> His daily life was of a curious microscopic sort, his whole world being limited to a circuit of a few feet from his person. His familiars were creeping and winged things, and they seemed to enroll him in their band. Bees hummed around his

[23] Hardy uses the adjective "vast" at least ten times in the course of the book (pp. 3, 15, 17, 59, 61, 187, 230, 385, 391, 458), besides such synonyms as "great," "huge," "enormous," "immense," "colossal" (pp. 6, 353, 420), "Ti-tanic" (p. 4), and "Atlantean" (p. 13).

ears . . . butterflies . . . quivered in the breath of his lips
. . . grasshoppers leaped over his feet. . . . Huge flies . . .
buzzed about him without knowing that he was a man. In
and out of the fern-dells snakes glided . . . young rabbits
came out from their forms to sun themselves. . . . None of
them feared him.[24]   (pp. 298–99)

These microscopic perspectives are closely related to Burke's
next category, INFINITY: "the ideas of eternity, and infinity, are
among the most affecting we have" (II, IV). Perspectives of infinite
space and infinite time are among Hardy's hallmarks. Eustacia's
attempt to escape her "lot" initially takes the form of challenging
space and time by means of her grandfather's telescope (pp. 62,
82, 102, 178, 401) and her grandmother's hourglass, which she
carries about with her, although Hardy assures us that she had a
watch (pp. 63, 79, 82, 142, 235).

The heath is the infinite setting of the action. To one standing
on it, "the distant rims of the world and of the firmament seemed
to be a division in time no less than a division in matter" (p. 3),
and Hardy speaks of its, rather than the world's, "nightly roll into
darkness" (p. 4), for it *is* the world of the book and therefore directly related to infinite space. The heath also suggests infinite
time:

> Every night its Titanic form seemed to await something; but
> it had waited thus, unmoved, during so many centuries,
> through the crises of so many things, that it could only be
> imagined to await one last crisis—the final overthrow.
>
> (p. 4; cf. p. 384)

Whereas its future is bound only by that usual *terminus ad quem*

---

[24] In reducing this paragraph to its essentials, I have omitted eighteen of its
twenty-eight lines of prose. The complete paragraph is much more vivid.

of the tragic vision, "the final overthrow," its historical past is traced to "the last geological change" (p. 7). Rainbarrow was built by "forgotten Celtic tribes" (pp. 455, 13). The heath has been the scene of "festival fires to Thor and Woden . . . Druidical rites and Saxon ceremonies" (p. 17). It bears witness to the Roman occupation (p. 7), and in autumn it recalls Caesar's annual anxiety to leave Britain (p. 60). It can still be described as it was in the Domesday Book and later by John Leland (p. 6), for it "had been from prehistoric times as unaltered as the stars overhead" (p. 7). At one point Clym finds himself *in* a prehistoric era:

> The ferny vegetation round him . . . was a grove of machine-made foliage, a world of green triangles with saw-edges, and not a single flower. The air was warm with a vaporous warmth, and the stillness was unbroken. Lizards, grasshoppers, and ants were the only living things to be beheld. The scene seemed to belong to the ancient world of the carboniferous period, when the forms of plants were few, and of the fern kind; when there was neither bud nor blossom, nothing but a monotonous extent of leafage, amid which no bird sang.
>
> (p. 241)

Civilization is the enemy of the heath (p. 6, 17); the few human remnants on and in it demonstrate the insignificance of man in Hardy's universe.[25] It is "obsolete" (p. 6), having "slipped out of its century generations ago" (p. 205). Diggory Venn, the spirit of the heath, belongs, like "the dodo . . . in the world of animals," to "a class rapidly becoming extinct . . . in the rural world" (p. 9). Hardy's assertions of the traditionalism and even paganism of

---

[25] See D. H. Lawrence, "Six Novels of Thomas Hardy . . . ," p. 53: Egdon "cannot be futile, for it is eternal. What is futile is the purpose of men."

the peasants, unaffected by Victorian change, are demonstrated in their performances of ancient seasonal rites—the November bonfires against winter (pp. 17–18), the Christmas mumming (pp. 143–47, 157–59), the Maypole (p. 459)—and rites of passage (p. 23), to say nothing of Susan Nunsuch's rites against witchcraft.

Whereas Burke's categories thus far have dealt primarily with visual perception, his final categories, two of which are particularly important for Hardy, deal with the other senses. The two which Hardy employs are the auditory and the tactile, treated by Burke as SOUND and BODILY PAIN. Among sounds conducive to "sublimity," Burke cites excessive loudness, such as the "noise of vast cataracts, raging storms, thunder" (II, xvii), "the fall of waters . . . [which roar] in the imagination long after the first sounds have ceased to affect it" (II, viii), sudden and unexpected sounds (II, xviii), "low, tremulous, intermitting" sounds of uncertain origin (II, xix), and "such sounds as imitate the natural inarticulate voices of men, or any animals in pain or danger" (II, xx).

I have already mentioned Hardy's storms and need adduce here only Eustacia's most terrible screech" (p. 209) in church and the roaring of Shadwater Weir at the catastrophe (p. 439). More interesting is Hardy's use of low, intermittent sounds, analogous to the microscopic visual perspective, for ominous effects. These are mainly associated with "the linguistic peculiarity of the heath" (p. 60), "a shrivelled and intermittent recitative" resulting from the "united products of infinitesimal vegetable causes" (pp. 60–61)—"the mummied heath-bells of the past summer":

So low was an individual sound from these that a combination of hundreds only just emerged from silence. . . . Yet scarcely a single accent among the many afloat to-night could have such power to impress a listener with thoughts of its origin. One inwardly saw the infinity of those combined multitudes; and perceived that each of the tiny trumpets was seized on, entered, scoured, and emerged from by the wind as thoroughly as if it were as vast as a crater.   (p. 61)

The "ideal of bodily pain," writes Burke, "is productive of the sublime, and nothing else in this sense [i.e., "feeling"] can produce it" (II, xxii). Hardy writes much of pain, although chiefly of mental or spiritual suffering or in metaphor. Actual bodily pain occurs only when Eustacia is pricked by Susan Nunsuch's stocking-needle "that deep that the maid fainted away" (p. 209), when she cuts her hand on the well-rope (p. 218), and when Mrs. Yeobright is bitten by the adder (pp. 347 ff., 360 f.). The chief image of pain is one of being stung, bitten, pierced, or impaled. The banks around Cap'n Vye's house are "bare of hedge, save such as was formed by disconnected tufts of furze, standing upon stems along the top, like impaled heads above a city wall" (p. 64). After his mother's death, Clym's thoughts "go through [him] like swords" (p. 366). On the night of Eustacia's death, Susan Nunsuch, who had actually pierced Eustacia once, makes an image of her and thrusts pins into it "in all directions, with apparently excruciating energy":

> Probably as many as fifty were thus inserted, some into the head of the wax model, some into the shoulders, some into the trunk, some upwards through the soles of the feet, till the figure was completely permeated with pins.   (p. 424) [26]

[26] This use of "permeated" is characteristic of Hardy's diction at its most imprecise; he had used the word appropriately at least twice before in the book in connection with Venn (p. 9) and with Clym (p. 205).

Meanwhile Thomasin like Eustacia is crossing the heath in the storm: "the rain flew in a level flight without sensible descent . . . and individual drops struck into her like the arrows into Saint Sebastian" (pp. 432–33). At the end of the book, Clym sometimes thinks "that he and his had been sarcastically and pitilessly handled in having such irons thrust into their souls" (p. 455; cf. p. 158).

Only one important category of Hardy's devices for effecting Burkean "sublimity"—Hardy adds a few of his own—has not yet been treated, the grotesque. It is not directly discussed in Part Two of the *Enquiry,* but in Part Three, on the "beautiful," there is a passage that suggests it. Burke is discussing the opposite of beauty:

> Ugliness I imagine . . . to be consistent enough with an idea of the sublime. But I would by no means insinuate that ugliness of itself is a sublime idea, unless united with such qualities as excite a strong terror. (III, xxi)

Any use Hardy makes of UGLINESS is united, at least by juxtaposition, with other qualities that Burke recognizes as sublime. Of the major characters, Venn, Hardy's "Mephistophelian visitant" (p. 89) in this book,[27] is a grotesque. He is "an instance of the pleasing being wasted to form the ground-work of the singular, when an ugly foundation would have done just as well for that purpose" (p. 90; cf. Clym's "singularity," pp. 162, 198). Various grotesque episodes stress his function as an agent of destiny, more specifically as the spirit of the heath—notably his apparent burrowing under-

[27] See J. O. Bailey's highly suggestive article, "Hardy's 'Mephistophelian Visitants,' " *PMLA,* LXI (1946), 1146–84. Venn was conceived as a "providential" spirit of the heath, as Hardy's note indicates: "He was to have retained his isolated and weird character to the last, and to have disappeared mysteriously from the heath" (p. 473).

ground, with a large pair of turves covering him, in order to get close enough to eavesdrop on Eustacia and Wildeve. His very name connects him with the heath; Diggory, a standard tag-name for an agricultural laborer, suggests one aspect of his occupation, while the word "venn" once had the meaning "mud, clay, dirt" (*O. E. D.* Fen *sb.*[1] 2).

Besides other grotesqueries, one in particular identifies the peasants, like Venn, with the heath: "Every individual was so involved in furze by his method of carrying the faggots that he appeared like a bush on legs till he had thrown them down" (p. 15), and around the flickering bonfire "those whom Nature had depicted as merely quaint became grotesque, the grotesque became preternatural; for all was in extremity" (p. 18).

I have unraveled a number of developed images and recurrent motifs by using Burke's *Enquiry* as a guidebook. To reweave them as Hardy wrote them—by rereading, first of all, the opening chapter on the heath and the chapter on Eustacia as "Queen of Nights" —is to understand more clearly, in Albert Guérard's words, "the large methods [Hardy] used to evoke the totality of Egdon Heath" and his "attempt to create personality through grandiose impressionism." [28] But Hardy was after bigger game; he aimed directly at two commonly associated qualities, the sublime and the tragic. He managed to attain his first goal, at whatever price, and almost attained his second. The very names for these qualities are keywords in the diction of his book and deserve some scrutiny. Consider the following description *cum* meditation from the notorious opening chapter:

[28] *Thomas Hardy: The Novels and Stories* (Cambridge, Mass., 1949), p. 138.

Twilight combined with the scenery of Egdon Heath to evolve a thing *majestic* without severity, *impressive* without showiness, emphatic in its admonitions, *grand* in its simplicity. The qualifications which frequently invest the façade of a prison with far more *dignity* than is found in the façade of a palace double its size lent to this heath a *sublimity* in which spots renowned for *beauty* of the accepted kind are utterly wanting. . . . Haggard Egdon appealed to a subtler and scarcer instinct, to a more recently learnt emotion, than that which responds to the sort of *beauty* called charming or fair.

Indeed, it is a question if the exclusive reign of this *orthodox beauty* is not approaching its last quarter. . . . The time seems near, if it has not actually arrived, when the chastened *sublimity* of a moor, a sea, or a mountain will be all of nature that is absolutely in keeping with the moods of *the more think-ing among mankind.* (pp. 4–5, italics added)

Burke's obvious preference for the sublime has become Hardy's invidious comparison (cf. p. 197). Neither the heath's nor Eusta-cia's beauty (pp. 106, 77) is of the orthodox kind. Hardy's descrip-tion of the heath as "impressive without showiness" and "grand in its simplicity" sounds suspiciously like his own program as a stylist. If it was, his pretensions often betray his intentions when we look at his style locally—as, for example, in the frequent ped-antry of his numerous allusions to the Bible, Shakespeare, classical mythology, and western European painters (to say nothing of Burke's blind men), which are often showy rather than functional. When the peasants' bonfire dissociates the top of Rainbarrow from the rest of the heath and Hardy writes that "the whole black phe-nomenon beneath represented Limbo as viewed from the brink by the sublime Florentine" (p. 17), we feel that this elegantly varied evocation of Dante is presumptuous as well as pretentious. Hardy is straining for his effect, and "sublimity," along with its near-synonyms "majesty," "grandeur," and "solemnity," in their various forms, occur frequently in the book, usually associated with the heath and Eustacia (for example, pp. 73, 81, 123, 217), though in one impressive instance at the end of the book with Clym's dead mother: she is, he thinks, a "sublime saint whose radiance even his tenderness for Eustacia could not obscure" (p. 483).

Hardy's rejection of orthodox beauty in favor of sublimity itself suggests that he aimed at "tragedy." The word obtrudes awkwardly upon the reader, as though Hardy were trying to guarantee the success of his intention by labeling it. Eustacia has "a pale, tragic face" (p. 373) and sighs "that tragic sigh of hers" (p. 172). Clym's encounter with his dying mother is called "The Tragic Meeting of Two Old Friends" (p. 344). On the night of Eustacia's death, the storm breathes "into the chimney strange low utterances that seemed to be the prologue to some tragedy" (p. 431). The heath itself suggests "tragical possibilities" (p. 6). As for Clym—and here Hardy's aim is painfully explicit—"if he were making a tragical figure in the world, so much the better for a narrative" (p. 198).

Despite his plain intention, and despite his use of many of the appurtenances of tragedy, Hardy does not succeed in this book in creating tragedy in any traditional sense. The major obstacles are that he does not have a hero of sufficient stature—an obstacle made greater by the facts that Eustacia is first groomed for the role (as scapegoat of isolated, romantic beauties) and Clym is later assigned it (as scapegoat for "advanced thinkers"; pp. 203, 161–62), and that this "hero" comes to no meaningful recognition of his relation to Hardy's universe. (Eustacia does come to such a recognition and commits suicide.) Yet there remain, as Guérard remarks, "the impression and overtones of tragedy." [29] Hardy's fiction is dominated by his need to demonstrate "the satire of Heaven" (p. 305), to show that Clym and those nearest him "had been sarcastically and pitilessly handled" (p. 455).[30] Virginia Woolf maintained that Hardy was "the greatest tragic writer among English novelists," [31] but in *The Return of the Native,* at least, the persistent overtones of traditional tragedy are consistently denied by Hardy's insistent irony.

I have, thus far, been treating Hardy's style primarily as recurrent patterning and as direct aiming at effects. Hardy would accuse me of "lack of whole-seeing," of being the kind of critic who judges "the landscape by a nocturnal exploration with a flash-lantern," or who, in his architectural image, scrutinizes "the tool-marks and [is] blind to the building. . . ." [32] Like any piece of architecture, the building must have a style and effects of its own, or to translate Hardy's metaphor, a fiction must be seen as a specimen of its proper genre and its effects must not be condemned because they are the effects of that genre rather than another. George Moore's mistake in his attacks on Hardy as "one of George Eliot's miscarriages" is that he assumes that Hardy was trying to write realistic novels of manners. Although Hardy himself clas-

[29] Introduction to *The Return of the Native* (New York, 1950), p. xix.

[30] Hardy's commitment to elegant variation sometimes leads him to use carelessly imprecise diction. In both of these comments, he means "irony" but is willing to use "satire" and "sarcasm" as though they were its exact synonyms.

[31] *The Common Reader,* II (New York, 1948), p. 276.

[32] "Apology" prefacing *Late Lyrics and Earlier* (1922), in *Collected Poems* (New York, 1946), p. 530.

sified half of his prose fictions, including all of the major ones, as "Novels of Character and Environment," his other two categories, "Romances and Fantasies" and "Novels of Ingenuity," suggest more nearly what they are—ironic romance. That is their "style," in the largest sense of the word, the frame of their worlds, their perspective on "reality" which requires that the reader take a particular stance in order to see them at their best.

In order to clarify this point, I shall draw upon Northrop Frye's brilliant organization of insights, *Anatomy of Criticism*. In terms of his treatment of "romance," Mrs. Yeobright is the Lady of Duty, "the sybilline wise mother-figure" ("She had a singular insight into life"), "who sits quietly at home waiting for the hero to finish his wanderings and come back to her." Eustacia is both the Lady of Pleasure and "the siren or beautiful witch." Hardy contrasts her with Thomasin in the "very common convention of the nineteenth-century novel" that uses two heroines, one dark, passionate (Hardy's word is "perfervid" [pp. 139, 169]), and somehow foreign, the other light, innocent, and sweet, just as he also uses the common device of making the Lady of Duty the mother-in-law of the Lady of Pleasure. Wildeve is the hero's opposite, the "traitor." And Venn partakes of the functions of the "magician who affects the action he watches over" and the servant or friend of the hero, who both retains "the inscrutability of [his] origin" and imparts "the mysterious rapport with nature that so often marks the central figure of romance." [33]

Ironic romance, however, shifts the emphasis from the central figure who is *en rapport* with nature to one who is antipathetic to

[33] *Anatomy of Criticism*, (Princeton, New Jersey, 1957), pp. 195–97, 101.

it. Eustacia is Hardy's protagonist, Clym but a secondary figure in Hardy's would-be "tragedy." [34] As Frye puts it,

> As tragedy moves over towards irony, the sense of inevitable event begins to fade out, and the sources of catastrophe come into view. In irony catastrophe is either arbitrary and meaningless, the impact of an unconscious (or, in the pathetic fallacy, malignant) world on conscious man [as in Hardy], or the result of more or less definable social and psychological forces [as in Ibsen].[35]

Eustacia and her "lot" are devised to win our "admiration" (I use the word to mean the rhetorical effect *admiratio*) for her defiance of her fate. Like the heath, which had "defied the cataclysmal onsets of centuries" (p. 384), she defies the "world" of the book. Her "smouldering rebelliousness" (p. 77) is associated with the "Promethean rebelliousness" (p. 18) of the November 6 bonfires. Just before the turning-point of the plot, Clym tells her that he can "rebel, in high Promethean fashion, against the gods and fate as well as you" (p. 302), but his "elastic mind" (p. 301) is not capable of Eustacia's kind of defiance as it does not measure up to her vision of greatness (pp. 80, 422). In her last speech before her death, her final act of defiance, she exclaims: "How I have tried

---

[34] In February, 1878, Hardy wrote to Arthur Hopkins, who illustrated *The Return of the Native* for *Belgravia*, that "the order of importance of the characters is as follows—1 Clym Yeobright 2 Eustacia 3 Thomasin and the reddleman 4 Wildeve 5 Mrs Yeobright." Richard L. Purdy, *Thomas Hardy: A Bibliographical Study* (London, 1954), p. 26.

[35] *Anatomy of Criticism*, p. 285. See also Arthur Mizener's *"Jude the Obscure* as a Tragedy," *Southern Review*, VI (1940), 193–213, one of the essays in the "Thomas Hardy Centennial Issue," in which the essays of Blackmur, Porter, and Zabel, from which I have quoted, first appeared.

and tried to be a splendid woman, and how destiny has been against me! . . . I do not deserve my lot!" (p. 422)—the final outcry echoing the last words of Aeschylus' Prometheus.

Clym, on the other hand, acquiesces in his fate. Although the book develops numerous parallels between him and Oedipus, they are finally outweighed by the parallels with Christ, John the Baptist, and St. Paul (pp. 203, 207, 334, 368). Hardy emphasizes his age, still less than thirty-three, at the end of the book, and his sermons are called "Sermons on the Mount" (p. 484). But to acquiesce as readers in the comforting notion of some sort of Christian-Stoic endurance is to miss Hardy's irony. Here the paragraph Hardy took over from Burke to describe Mrs. Yeobright's *insight* connects thematically with the allusions to Oedipus. Eustacia is once compared with the Sphinx (p. 75), as Clym with Oedipus (p. 384), but he cannot cope with her riddle; she bewitches him. The Oedipus allusions are primarily associated with insight and blindness, and it is Eustacia, not Clym, who accurately "discerns" (one of Hardy's keywords) the nature of their world. Near the end of the book, Hardy writes that Clym

> did sometimes think he had been ill-used by fortune, so far as to say that to be born is a palpable dilemma, and that instead of men aiming to advance in life with glory they should calculate how to retreat out of it without shame. But that he and his had been sarcastically and pitilessly handled in having such irons thrust into their souls he did not maintain long.

And then Hardy baldly states the point of his irony:

> It is usually so, except with the sternest of men. Human beings, in their generous endeavour to construct a hypothesis that shall not degrade a First Cause, have always hesitated to

conceive a dominant power of lower moral quality than their
own; and, even while they sit down and weep by the waters
of Babylon, invent excuses for the oppression which prompts
their tears.   (p. 455)

Clym is not one of "the sternest of men"; unlike Eustacia, he cannot see that the universe Hardy contrived for his characters is
dominated by a power "of lower moral quality than their own."
The last words of the book drive the point home: "others . . .
remarked that it was well enough for a man to take to preaching
who could not see to do anything else" (p. 485, italics added).

Hardy labors to arouse in us a fearful "admiration" for Eustacia
and a pitiful sympathy for Clym; this very distinction implies a
world in which heroic tragedy is no longer possible. The terror
that Eustacia's fate arouses contrasts sharply with the pity, tinged
necessarily with some degree of contempt, we are brought to feel
for Clym. *The Return of the Native* is Hardy's version of *Hedda
Gabler,* for although Ibsen is a realist and Hardy a romancer, both
are ironists. In both works, the heroine is the centrally interesting
and, for all her faults, admirable figure, in revolt against the con-
ditions of her existence. Clym, though groomed for a more dignified role, becomes merely a more sympathetic Tesman. We are
led to expect no more from his sincere preachings and lectures "on
morally unimpeachable subjects" (p. 485) than from Tesman's
pedantic and derivative scholarship. To be sure, Hardy, unlike
Ibsen, pulled his punches, in deference presumably to his editor's
sense of what the readers of *Belgravia* would accept. But he appealed to other readers who have "an austere artistic code" (p.
473), readers who are "of the more thinking among mankind"
(p. 5) if not indeed "the sternest of men" (p. 455). His style as

ironist was cramped by the demands of serial publication, but irony is, at length, his strongest and most consistent style, and the evocation of the sublime, albeit in the ironic mode, is one of his most powerful effects.

G. Armour Craig

On the Style of *Vanity Fair*

... there is still a very material difference of opinion as to the
real nature and character of the Measure of Value in this country.
My first question, therefore, is, what constitutes this Measure of
Value? What is the signification of that word 'a Pound'?

Speech of Sir Robert Peel on the Bank Charter Acts (6 May 1844)

Perhaps I might be a heroine still, but I shall never be a good
woman, I know.

Mrs. Gaskell, *Wives and Daughters* (1866)

"Among all our novelists his style is the purest, as to my ears
it is also the most harmonious. Sometimes it is disfigured by
a slight touch of affectation, by little conceits which smell of
the oil;—but the language is always lucid." The judgment is
Anthony Trollope's and the lucidity he praises is Thackeray's:
"The reader, without labour, knows what he means, and knows
all that he means." [1] The judgment has been shared by many,
perhaps even by Thackeray himself, for he was vigilant in
detecting "fine writing" or "claptraps" in the work of others,[2]

[1] *An Autobiography*, ed. by Frederick Page (London, 1950), p. 244.

[2] See, e.g., his review of "A New Spirit Of The Age," *Works—The Oxford
Thackeray*, ed. by George Saintsbury (17 vols.; London, 1908), VI, 424; or some
advice on "fine writing" in *The Letters and Private Papers of William Makepeace
Thackeray*, ed. by Gordon N. Ray (4 vols.; Cambridge, Mass., 1945), II, 192.

and for himself he insisted that "this person writing strives to tell the truth. If there is not that, there is nothing." [3] Yet some reconciling is necessary, for the truth is not always lucid and lucidity may not always be quite true.

There is at any rate a passage in chapter 42 of *Vanity Fair* [4] for Trollope's judgment of which the modern reader—at least this reader—would give a good deal. It describes the life of Jane Osborne keeping house for her father: her sister is now the fashionable Mrs. Frederick Bullock, her brother, disowned by their father for his marriage to Amelia Sedley, has been killed at Waterloo, and Jane now lives in idle spinsterhood in the great glum house in Russell Square.

> It was an awful existence. She had to get up of black winter's mornings to make breakfast for her scowling old father, who would have turned the whole house out of doors if his tea had not been ready at half-past eight. She remained silent opposite to him, listening to the urn hissing, and sitting in tremor while the parent read his paper, and consumed his accustomed portion of muffins and tea. At half-past nine he rose and went to the City, and she was almost free till dinner-time, to make visitations in the kitchen and to scold the servants: to drive abroad and descend upon the tradesmen, who were prodigiously respectful: to leave her cards and her papa's at the great glum respectable houses of their City friends; or to sit alone in the large drawing-room, expecting visitors; and working at a huge piece of worsted by the fire, on the sopha, hard by the great Iphigenia clock,

[3] Preface to *Pendennis*.

[4] References are to the Modern Library College Editions reprint (New York, 1950), which is based on the edition of 1864.

which ticked and tolled with mournful loudness in the dreary room. The great glass over the mantle-piece, faced by the other great console glass at the opposite end of the room, increased and multiplied between them the brown holland bag in which the chandelier hung; until you saw these brown holland bags fading away in endless perspectives, and this apartment of Miss Osborne's seemed the centre of a system of drawing-rooms. When she removed the cordovan leather from the grand piano, and ventured to play a few notes on it, it sounded with a mournful sadness, startling the dismal echoes of the house.   (pp. 441–42)

Thackeray's prose is seldom better than this. The passage comes from a paragraph that comments on the difference between Jane Osborne's life and that of her sister: "One can fancy the pangs" with which Jane regularly read about Mrs. Frederick Bullock in the "Morning Post," particularly the account of her presentation at the Drawing-room. The reader, characteristically, is invited to supply from his own observation the sort of vulgar envy that feeds upon accounts of "Fashionable Reunions" in the newspaper and to look down on Jane Osborne's suffering as no more than the deprivation of the snobbish pleasures of elegant society. The passage begins, then, easily enough: "It was an awful existence." And "awful" is at first simply a colloquial affectation. It becomes something more, however, as we move into the account of Jane's routine and ascend from the tremors of the breakfast table to the solitude of the drawing room with its covered chandelier "fading away in endless perspectives": the conversational pitch turns momentarily solemn with the vision of "this apartment of Miss Osborne's" as "the centre of a system of drawing-rooms"—including perhaps even that most august of all such apartments where her sister has been received. It would be hard to find this an example of the "little conceits which smell of the oil," for even here Thackeray does not lose his customary confidential hold upon the reader. The vision is kept close to us by his usual resource: the opposing mirrors "increased and multiplied between them the brown holland bag in which the chandelier hung; until *you* saw these brown holland bags fading away in endless perspectives." The "you" is no doubt as unobtrusive as an idiom. But it is not inconsistent with Thackeray's constant and fluent address to his reader, an address at its best as easy as idiom. In this very short passage Thackeray has moved from an example of the snobbery he loved to detect to a memorable symbol of the society in which snobbery flourishes. It is a society of endless perspectives, a system of drawing rooms whose center is everywhere, whose circumference is nowhere.

But is this what Thackeray meant? And is it the "all" that he meant? Certainly the symbol is not characteristic—it is indeed unique in *Vanity Fair*. Usually, or at any rate perhaps too often, Thackeray renders the barren routines of high life in mock genealogies or in the kind of mildly allegorical guest list that follows this passage. We are told that twice a month the solitary dinners of Mr. and Miss Osborne are shared with "Old Dr. Gulp and his lady from Bloomsbury Square, . . . old Mr. Frowser the attorney, . . . old Colonel Livermore, . . . old Serjeant Toffy, . . . sometimes old Sir Thomas Coffin." *Vanity Fair,* we recall, began as "Pen and Pencil Sketches of English

Society," as an extension of *The Book Of Snobs*. Yet Thackeray seems to have felt the need of some larger, more inclusive presiding idea. In the early stages of writing the first few numbers he "ransacked" his brain for another title, and "Vanity Fair," he said, came to him suddenly in the middle of the night.[5] It seems to have summed up for him a position from which he could confidently go on with his "Novel without a Hero," but a position of course very different from John Bunyan's. The original Vanity Fair as described by Evangelist is the dwelling place of abominations. But it is after all only one more obstacle on the road to the Celestial City, and all such obstacles are rewards in disguise. "He that shall die there," says Evangelist, "although his death will be unnatural, and his pain perhaps great, he will yet have the better of his fellow." While there are some unnatural and painful deaths in Thackeray's Fair, there seems to be no act of resistance or sacrifice by which anyone can get the better of anyone else, and the irony of the title has no doubt been lively in the minds of many readers. But Evangelist lays down a more poignantly ironical prescription: "he that will go to the [Celestial] City, and yet not go through this Town [where Vanity Fair is kept], *must* needs *go out of the World*."[6] If there is no Celestial City beyond Thackeray's Fair, and if there is no hero determined to fight on to a heavenly peak, it is even more certain that none of Thackeray's characters shall go out of this world. On every page of *Vanity Fair* we

[5] Gordon N. Ray, *Thackeray: The Uses of Adversity: 1811–1846* (New York, 1955), pp. 384–85.

[6] *The Pilgrim's Progress* . . . , ed. by Edmund Venables, rev. by Mabel Peacock (Oxford, 1925), pp. 82 ff.

find description, exposure, comment, from a position much less elevated and secure than that of an evangelist, yet one from which we do see into an "all" as large as a whole society.

Certainly the style of all this commenting and exposing is this-worldly to a degree that would have puzzled Bunyan as much as it has troubled some of his descendants. In the preface to *Pendennis* Thackeray speaks of his work as "a sort of confidential talk between reader and writer," and it was the excess of this conception of himself—"the little earmark by which he is most conspicuous"—that Trollope found "his most besetting sin in style." The "sin" is "a certain affected familiarity": Thackeray "indulges too frequently in little confidences with individual readers, in which pretended allusions to himself are frequent. 'What would you do? what would you say now, if you were in such a position?' he asks." [7] Yet for Trollope, although this familiarity might breed occasional contempt, it did not finally compromise the great virtue of Thackeray's lucidity. "As I have said before, the reader always understands his words without an effort, and receives all that the author has to give." [8] But to know what, and to know all, a writer means is to be in his confidence indeed, and it would be a serious lapse of style that this confidence should break down in affectation or something worse.

In "Before the Curtain," the preface he wrote in 1848 for the completed novel, Thackeray promises his reader "no other moral than this tag to the present story," that after wandering with him through the Fair, "When you come home, you sit down,

[7] Anthony Trollope, *Thackeray* (London, 1879), pp. 197–98.
[8] *Ibid.*, p. 198.

in a sober, contemplative, not uncharitable frame of mind, and apply yourself to your books or your business." He raises no literary expectations, he promises no carefully graduated feast of human nature, he does not even excuse himself to those who find all Fairs "immoral" and hence refuse to enter this one. The stern moralists may be quite right in withholding their custom, but those "of a lazy, or a benevolent, or a sarcastic mood, may perhaps like to step in for half an hour and look at the performance." This casualness, the queer juxtaposition of "lazy," "benevolent," and "sarcastic," may seem like the very height of good breeding. It does sum up the uncomfortable collocation of responses that any reader must make to some stretches of the novel. But it also promises that this writer will keep us free from violent emotions as we read. It is the guarantee of a special detachment.

Such detachment is often suggested by a coy version of one of Fielding's comic devices. When we witness the departure of Becky and Amelia from Chiswick Mall, the last flurry of farewells is recounted thus: "Then came the struggle and the parting below. Words refuse to tell it. . . ." The congregation of servants and pupils, the hugging and kissing and crying are such "as no pen can depict, and as the tender heart would fain pass over" (chap. 1, p. 6). Or, on the morning after the fatal excursion to Vauxhall, Joseph Sedley lies "groaning in agonies which the pen refuses to describe" (chap. 6, p. 55) while he suffers the aftermath of rack punch. Becky, disappointed in her attempt to capture Joseph, goes away from the Sedley house to her duties as governess: "Finally came the parting with Amelia, over which I intend to throw a veil" (chap. 6, p. 61).

Such mild affectations as these amuse a good deal less than their frequency suggests they should, however obliquely they may glance at sentimental explorations of young female affection or the tract-writer's interest in the heavy repentance of the drunkard. But they are the simplest and the least interesting form of a larger kind of detachment.

About other episodes the narrator is more artfully silent. Perhaps the most interesting is the courtship of Rawdon Crawley, which extends over several chapters and is concealed in the narrative of Becky's ministrations to old Miss Crawley. It will be recalled that the success of Becky's attentions to this lady, the old aunt whose wealth is the object of all the Crawleys' envy and scheming, alarm Mrs. Bute Crawley—whose portrait, incidentally, as well as that of her family and of her husband the Rector, make one wonder that Thackeray could have quarreled with Jerrold's anticlericalism.[9] Mrs. Bute's scheming to secure Miss Crawley's money for her own leads her to warn Rawdon that when his stepmother dies, old Sir Pitt will marry Becky. Rawdon's response sets the level of intrigue exactly:

'By Jove, it's too bad," thought Rawdon, "too bad, by Jove! I do believe the woman wants the poor girl to be ruined, in order that she shouldn't come into the family as Lady Crawley."   (chap. 14, p. 133)

He proceeds to the recommended seduction, but is outguessed by the frank and outraged role that Becky adopts when he "rallie[s] her in his graceful way about his father's attachment." The game goes on, Miss Crawley recovers from her surfeit under Becky's assiduous care, and shortly news comes that the

[9] See Ray, *Uses of Adversity,* pp. 370–71.

meek Lady Crawley is dead. Rawdon and his aunt discuss the matter while Becky stands by.

> Rebecca said nothing. She seemed by far the gravest and most impressed of the family. She left the room before Rawdon went away that day; but they met by chance below, as he was going away after taking leave, and had a parley together.   (chap. 14, p. 143)

And the next thing we know, old Sir Pitt has come to town and is down on his knees to ask for the hand of Becky. The narrator comments:

> In the course of this history we have never seen her lose her presence of mind; but she did now, and wept some of the most genuine tears that ever fell from her eyes.
>   (chap. 14, p. 144)

But what does "genuine" mean here? Or "they met by chance" in the passage above? Are we to infer that during their "parley" Becky uses the threat of a proposal from the father to make sure of the son? Are we to infer that the tears are genuine because she has planned too well—the threat she has used to get one husband has turned out to be prophetic, and she might have had the father? Are they tears of rage? of regret? As we move on to the next chapter we certainly find no circumstantial report of when and how Becky and Rawdon are married; instead there is a good deal of indirect veiling of the scene and refusing of the pen. "How they were married is not of the slightest consequence to anybody." Perhaps, it is conjectured, they went off one afternoon when Becky was presumed to be visiting Amelia. But the matter is left in uncertainty. On the one hand, "Who needs to be told, that if a woman has a will, she will assuredly find a way?" And on the other: "who on earth, after the daily experience we have, can question the probability of a gentleman marrying anybody?" (chap. 16, p. 153).

The concealment of the circumstances of the marriage may appeal to the lazy, may satisfy the benevolent, and it may give the sarcastic something to work on too. But its most important effect is that the narration here, clustered about with confidential comments and dismissive questions, sets before us a way of knowing the world. It is a way so inferential, so dependent upon unfinished implications, that it comes close to the character of gossip. And a good gossip, while its unfinished sentences and its discreet and indiscreet omissions may keep us from the exhilaration of indignation or rhapsody, can suggest values and insights superior to the vocabulary of the purveyor or the listener. Here, whatever the meaning of that "by chance" that modifies the meeting of Becky and Rawdon, or whatever the meaning of that "genuine" that modifies her tears, we can only infer that the marriage is the result neither of grand passion nor of mean seduction. The veiling of the secret here means that we can only accept Becky's marriage as a convenience. Even the grossness of Mrs. Bute's plotting is lost in the shadows.

The questions with which Thackeray disposes of this affair —"Who needs to be told . . . who can question the probability . . ."—are of course the most conspicuous earmark of his detachment in *Vanity Fair*. There is the issue of who made the first move in Becky's first romance, with the young Reverend Mr. Crisp who came infatuated to tea at Chiswick Mall: after a parenthetical cloud of hints and counter-hints the narrator concludes, "But who can tell you the real truth of the matter?"

(chap. 2, p. 14). Just as when the pen refuses to tell, the implication here is only coy. But a good many hundred pages later, in what is called "A Vagabond Chapter" (chap. 64), this kind of coyness can exasperate. It comes in a passage summarizing Becky's career after her fall from polite society in London: "When she got her money she gambled; when she had gambled it she was put to shifts to live; who knows how or by what means she succeeded? . . . The present historian can give no certain details regarding the event" (p. 681). The detachment inculcated here is vast and affluent indeed; it is perhaps matched only by the elaborate veiling of the circumstances of Joseph Sedley's death. But the most puzzling questions in the book are those that comment upon its crucial passage.

Every reader of *Vanity Fair* remembers the "discovery scene" of chapter 53—the scene in which Becky suffers exposure and isolation after her husband and Lord Steyne violently clash. And every student of the novel knows that this scene is a battleground upon which the judgments of a number of Thackeray's critics have collided. Rawdon, having been freed from the spunging house, hurries "across the streets and the great squares of Vanity Fair, and bursts in upon his wife and Lord Steyne in something less than *flagrante delicto* though ready for embarrassment."

> Steyne was hanging over the sofa on which Becky sate. The wretched woman was in a brilliant full toilette, her arms and all her fingers sparkling with bracelets and rings; and the brilliants on her breast which Steyne had given her. He had her hand in his, and was bowing over it to kiss it, when Becky started up with a faint scream as she caught

sight of Rawdon's white face. At the next instant she tried a smile, a horrid smile, as if to welcome her husband; and Steyne rose up, grinding his teeth, pale, and with fury in his looks.

He, too, attempted a laugh—and come forward holding out his hand. "What, come back! How d'ye do, Crawley?" he said, the nerves of his mouth twitching as he tried to grin at the intruder.

There was that in Rawdon's face which caused Becky to fling herself before him. "I am innocent, Rawdon," she said; "before God, I am innocent." She clung hold of his coat, of his hands; her own were all covered with serpents, and rings, and baubles.

"I am innocent. —Say I am innocent," she said to Lord Steyne.

He thought a trap had been laid for him, and was as furious with the wife as with the husband. "You innocent! Damn you!" he screamed out. "You innocent! Why, every trinket you have on your body is paid for by me. I have given you thousands of pounds which this fellow has spent, and for which he has sold you. Innocent, by—! You're as innocent as your mother, the ballet-girl, and your husband the bully. Don't think to frighten me as you have done others. Make way, sir, and let me pass"; and Lord Steyne seized up his hat, and, with flame in his eyes, and looking his enemy fiercely in the face, marched upon him, never for a moment doubting that the other would give way.

But Rawdon Crawley springing out, seized him by the neckcloth, until Steyne, almost stangled, writhed, and bent under his arm. "You lie, you dog"! said Rawdon. "You lie, you coward and villain!" And he struck the Peer twice over the face with his open hand, and flung him bleeding to the ground. It was all done before Rebecca could interpose. She stood there trembling before him. She admired her husband, strong, brave, and victorious.

"Come here," he said. —She came up at once.

"Take off those things." —She began, trembling, pulling the jewels from her arms, and the rings from her shaking fingers, and held them all in a heap, quivering, and looking up at him. "Throw them down," he said, and she dropped them. He tore the diamond ornament out of her breast, and flung it at Lord Steyne. It cut him on his bald forehead. Steyne wore the scar to his dying day.   (pp. 554-55)

The theatricality of the passage—Becky's clinging and quivering, the serpents and baubles on her hands, Rawdon's springing out and his terse manifesto, the flame in the eyes of the wicked nobleman and the lifelong scar on his head—all such features suggest that the creator of Punch's Prize novelists is once again engaged in something like parody.[10] On the other hand it has been asserted that far from a joke, the scene "is the chief ganglion of the tale; and the discharge of energy from Rawdon's fist [*sic*] is the reward and consolation of the reader." [11] The most extensive criticism of the scene finds it unprepared for and conveyed by a dramatic technique foreign to Thackeray's genius,[12]

---

[10] As has been suggested by Kathleen Tillotson, *Novels of the Eighteen-Forties* (Oxford, 1954), pp. 233-34.

[11] Robert Louis Stevenson, "A Gossip on Romance," *Memories and Portraits* (New York, 1910), p. 239 (Vol. 17 of the Biographical Edition of the *Works*). Stevenson's judgment is endorsed by Professor Ray in *Uses of Adversity,* p. 410.

[12] Percy Lubbock, *The Craft of Fiction* (London, 1954), pp. 101 ff. Lubbock's argument has been criticized by Professor Ray (*Uses of Adversity,* pp. 409-10) and by Geoffrey Tillotson, *Thackeray the Novelist* (Cambridge, 1954), pp. 82 ff.

but this judgment has in turn been disposed of by another critic who finds Thackeray's usual stamp upon it and some other felicities as well. He suggests that one of these is the way in which "Steyne wore the scar" echoes "Steyne wore the star." [13] By the same sort of reasoning we might infer from "He tore the diamond ornament out of her breast" that Becky's heart is surpassing hard; and certainly Thackeray tells us that the battle takes the heart out of her. But the one touch upon which Thackeray himself is known to have commented is Becky's response to the sudden burst of energy from Rawdon: "She stood there trembling before him. She admired her husband, strong, brave, and victorious." Of this observation Thackeray is reported to have said that it was a touch of genius,[14] and it does consort well with his special genius in the rest of the book.

For although the battle seems to be the expression of outraged honor, it is a collision that misses its main issue and prize. As the resistless masses meet, Becky stands off to one side, and although her admiration is unacceptable or even unknown to Rawdon, and although we are told that her life seems so "miserable, lonely, and profitless" after Rawdon has silently departed that she even thinks of suicide, there is still a profound irrelevance in this violent scene. Becky's maid comes upon her in her dejection and asks the question that is in every reader's mind: *"Mon Dieu,* madame, what has happened?" And the "person writing" concludes this crucial chapter with an enlargement of the same question:

[13] G. Tillotson, *Thackeray the Novelist,* p. 84.

[14] See Ray, *Uses of Adversity,* p. 500, n. 19; and *Letters and Private Papers,* II, 352n.

What *had* happened? Was she guilty or not? She said not; but who could tell what was truth which came from those lips; or if that corrupt heart was in this case pure? All her lies and her schemes, all her selfishness and her wiles, all her wit and her genius had come to this bankruptcy.   (p. 556) Becky lies down, the maid goes to the drawing room to gather up the pile of trinkets, and the chapter ends. If Thackeray has not risen to a cruel joke on those readers who find consolation and reward in the discharge of energy from Rawdon, he has at least interrupted their satisfaction.

Lord Steyne's meaning of "guilty"—"He thought a trap had been laid for him" by Becky and Rawdon—is of course quite false, though it corroborates the characterization of Steyne as one experienced in double-dealing. "Guilty" from Rawdon's point of view of course means, as he tells Pitt next day, that "it was a regular plan between that scoundrel and her" to get him out of the way (chap. 54, p. 559). And Thackeray goes to as great lengths to make it impossible for us to know that this interpretation is true as he does to conceal the timing and motives of Becky's marriage. To see the entangling and displacing of any clear answer, we need only ask "guilty of what?" The usual answer is of course "guilty of adultery" (or guilty of getting ready for it),[15] and Thackeray's silence is commonly attributed to his awareness of the "squeamishness" of his public. Indeed he himself lends real authority to this account of the matter. In 1840, writing on Fielding, he complains that the world no longer tolerates real satire. "The same vice exists now, only we don't speak about it; the same things are done, but

[15] See, e.g., Ray, *Uses of Adversity,* p. 502, n. 14.

we don't call them by their names." [16] And in *Vanity Fair* he complains that he must be silent about some events in Becky's later career because he must satisfy "the moral world, that has, perhaps, no particular objection to vice, but an insuperable repugnance to hearing vice called by its proper name" (chap. 64, p. 671). There may well be evidence in Thackeray's personal history to suggest in addition that he was, perhaps even before the separation from his mad wife, evasive and unclear on the subject of sexual behavior. But however complicated the tensions of Thackeray's own emotional experience, and however rigid the scruples of his audience, the answer to the questions with which he comments on this most important episode cannot be a single "name" or possess any "proper name." For he has led us here, however uneasily, with mingled attitudes of parody and outrage, to a startling though incomplete vision of a new social world, a vision exactly proportioned to the irrelevance of the violence we have witnessed.

The words of the passage that command our moral response are precisely those that most nearly approach parody: Becky responds to a nameless "that" in Rawdon's face by exclaiming "I am innocent." If the reader trained in melodrama scoffs at the response and turns Becky into a consummate villain, he will have some trouble getting through the rest of the novel, and it is likely that he will long since have become exasperated with Thackeray's tone, his silences and implications. The same is true, moreover, of the sentimental reader who throws down the volume and declares that Becky has been monstrously wronged and victimized by wicked men in a bad world. But the reader

[16] *Works,* III, 385.

who says, in effect, "it is impossible to tell whether or of what she is guilty" is exactly in the difficult position of one who accepts Thackeray's narrative as it is given. And what such a reader sees from this position must fill him with wonder if not dismay. For he sees that while he wants to answer these questions, he cannot do so, and he can only conclude that he is looking at a situation before which his moral vocabulary is irrelevant. Becky in her isolation has finally gone out of this world, and it will take a new casuistry to bring her back. Thackeray uses some strong moral words in his comment, it is true: "who could tell what was truth which came from those lips; or if that corrupt heart was in this case pure?" But while we know that Becky has lied heartily to Steyne, and to his hearty admiration, we cannot know that she is lying to Rawdon when she insists on her innocence. Whatever corruption we may have seen, the question this time is in earnest. The qualities named in the final statement, and especially by its last word, tell us where we are: "All her lies and her schemes, all her selfishness and her wiles, all her wit and her genius had come to this bankruptcy." For these are the terms not so much of moral as of financial enterprise, and "this bankruptcy" is the real touch of genius in the passage. Thackeray's questions and his comment express neither indignation nor sympathy. Rather, they bring before us the terrible irresolution of a society in which market values and moral values are discontinuous and separate. And Thackeray will not—he can not—support us as we revolt from such a spectacle.

The ghostly paradigm upon which human nature plays in *Vanity Fair* is the credit economy that in Thackeray's own lifetime finally developed from a money economy. Even the constant gambling in Thackeray's Fair, historically appropriate as it may be to his Regency setting (and much of his own early experience as it may reflect), suggests the unpredictability of the system. Distant though the gambler may be from respectability, his luck is only a little less mysterious than the power his winnings confer upon him. However it may be in the most famous conversation recorded in modern literary history, it is all too true in *Vanity Fair* that rich people are different because they have more money. Thackeray exposed himself to some high-minded criticism from George Henry Lewes when he published the number containing Becky's famous reflection, "I think I could be a good woman if I had five thousand a year." For he had commented, "And who knows but Rebecca was right in her speculations—and that it was only a question of money and fortune which made the difference between her and an honest woman?" (chap. 41, p. 436). In its interrogative form the comment is much more precise than the declaration Thackeray wrote to Lewes. The latter called it "detestable" to say that "honesty is only the virtue of abundance." Thackeray replied that he meant "only that he in the possession of luxuries . . . should be very chary of despising poor Lazarus on foot, and look very humbly and leniently upon the faults of his less fortunate brethren." This is of course no answer; or if it is, it asks for a curious forbearance towards Becky Sharp. But Thackeray qualifies at once: "I am quite aware of the dismal roguery . . . [which] goes all through the Vanity Fair story—and God forbid that the world should be like it altogether: though I fear it is more like it than we like to own." [17] The likeness to "the

---

[17] *Letters and Private Papers*, II, 353–54.

world" is in the belief that money is magic and in the frightening awareness, no doubt recently reinforced by the financial crisis of 1847, that no theory had yet been devised to control it. Walter Bagehot, in the *Economic Studies* he was composing in the 1870s, confessed to "a haze" in the language in which he described the growth of capital, and he remarked too with admiration that "a very great many of the strongest heads in England spend their minds on little else than on thinking whether other people will pay their debts."[18] For him that system was "marvellous" by which "an endless succession of slips of written promises should be turned into money as readily as if they were precious stones"— so marvelous indeed that it "would have seemed incredible in commerce till very recent times."[19] Thackeray's attitude, doubtless shaped by the short period he spent as a bill broker in 1833— an episode he apparently tried hard to forget[20]—was not so admiring. His Fair, at any rate, is a market the movements of which are perplexing in the extreme.

The first mention of the "guilt" or "innocence" of Becky's relations to Lord Steyne comes in a passage about the "awful kitchen inquisition" of the servants of Vanity Fair. We are told that Raggles, the retired butler of Miss Crawley, who owns the house in Curzon Street where Becky and Rawdon live well on nothing a year, is ruined by his extension of credit to them. But he is the victim of something more than the simple excess of liabilities over assets. The *"Vehmgericht* of the servants'-hall" early pronounces Becky guilty:

And I shame to say, she would not have got credit had they

<hr>

[18] *The Works and Life of Walter Bagehot,* ed. by Mrs. Russell Barrington (10 vols.; London, 1915), VII, 248, 131.

[19] *Ibid.,* p. 251.   [20] See *Uses of Adversity,* pp. 159–60.

not believed her to be guilty. It was the sight of the Marquis of Steyne's carriage-lamps at her door, contemplated by Raggles, burning in the blackness of midnight, "that kep him up," as he afterwards said; that, even more than Rebecca's arts and coaxings.   (chap. 44, pp. 461–62)

The question of guilt here is quite subordinate to the question of credit, and Raggles is ruined not because he is right about Becky's guilt but because he believes in a strict correlation between Becky's moral and financial status. The last of Raggles is seen at the drunken party of the servants on the morning after the battle; our last glimpse of him is not as he suffers in ruin but as he looks at his fellows "with a wild surprise" upon hearing from Becky that Rawdon "has got a good appointment" (chap. 55, p. 565). It is no wonder that Thackeray should have said in a letter to his mother written during the very month when the "discovery scene" appeared,

> I cant find the end of the question between property and labour. We want something almost equal to a Divine Person to settle it. I mean if there is ever to be an elucidation of the mystery it is to be solved by a preacher of such novelty and authority, as will awaken and convince mankind—but O how and when? [21]

Whatever the fate of the larger question, Thackeray does do some novel preaching upon bankruptcy in one section of *Vanity Fair*. John Sedley, we recall, is ruined in the uncertainties following Napoleon's escape from Elba (chap. 18, pp. 170 ff.), and Thackeray's extended portrait of the "business and bustle and mystery of a ruined man" (chap. 20, p. 195) seems at first

[21] *Letters and Private Papers*, II, 356.

sight disproportionate. Of course the bankruptcy accounts for the career of Amelia, but not for all of it. For old Osborne, who also emerges from the background just here, is described as behaving towards his former friend Sedley "with savageness and scorn." Our attitude is shaped precisely by Osborne's insisting that as a bankrupt Sedley must be wicked—that he is both out of business and out of the circle of decency. "From a mere sense of consistency, a persecutor is bound to show that the fallen man is a villain—otherwise he, the persecutor, is a wretch himself" (chap. 18, p. 173). And Osborne is characterized more grossly still by his opposition to Amelia for his son, by his insistence that George marry the rich mulatto Miss Schwarz, and by his vast self-righteousness. Osborne is perhaps an inept caricature of the City man who has succumbed completely to the superstitions of money, but he is a new kind of portrait, and one not less complicated than Dickens's portrait of another hard businessman whose adventures were being issued in installments at the same time.

While Thackeray's Mr. Osborne is a crude warning to those who identify bankruptcy and corruption, Dickens's Mr. Dombey is an astonishing testimonial to the degree of violence that must be exerted to link the experience of bankruptcy with moral reform. In the same month, March of 1848,[22] in which they read of the collision between Rawdon and Lord Steyne, readers who followed both authors were shaken by a passage of dreadful violence that describes a collision between Mr. Dombey's manager, Carker, and a railway engine (chap. 55). Dombey witnesses the event and faints at the sight—it is not an "accident"

[22] See K. Tillotson, *Novels of the Eighteen-Forties,* p. 318.

but the physical embodiment of a terrible obsession. When we next encounter Dombey (chap. 58) he is superintending the bankruptcy of his firm which results from Carker's secret machinations and which he will do nothing to avert. He is alone in the world, for he has driven away his gentle daughter Florence, and he is a "ruined man." With gruesome immediacy he thinks of suicide, but just before the knife strikes, his daughter rushes in, a great reconciliation and redemption occurs, and Mr. Dombey, no longer worth five thousand or very much of anything a year, is at last a good man. For all his inventive energy Dickens cannot make clear the relation between the departure of Carker from this world and the moral conversion that Mr. Dombey then undergoes. But this number of *Dombey and Son* together with the contemporaneous number of *Vanity Fair* suggests the extreme lengths to which two of the most sensitive minds of the mid-century were driven in their effort to reconcile the mysterious power of finance capitalism with the requirements of private morality. "Sell yourself" still meant the worst degradation, but the time was approaching when it would become a formula for "success."

In *Vanity Fair* at any rate Becky's bankruptcy offers no clearer connection between villainy—or goodness—and loss of credit than does the situation of Old John Sedley that Osborne so ruthlessly categorizes. The thoroughness with which Thackeray has covered his tracks suggests that no single transaction, not even payment by adultery, is at issue here. The kind of credit upon which the Crawleys lived so well in London and Paris is beyond the power of any act or value to overtake, for it is the social version of that system in which the perpetual promise to pay is taken for the perpetual fact of payment. "The truth is, when we say of a gentleman that he lives well on nothing a year, we use the word 'nothing' to signify something unknown" (chap. 36, p. 374). It may be that Rawdon and Becky are "wicked," but their wickedness will not account for their credit as they pursue the fashionable life. Just as the war that so mysteriously yet inevitably ruined John Sedley was, as Thackeray tells us, a lucky accident interrupting the endless double- and triple-dealing among nations (chap. 28, pp. 279–80), so for Becky an accident interrupts the double-dealing and counter double-dealing of the scramble for social power. The perspectives here are indeed almost endless; they are certainly beyond the limits of innocence or guilt. Even Rawdon, who experiences something like conversion or reform as Becky's career reaches its height, is not quite secure. His one assertion to Becky after the battle is an ironic fulfillment of Steyne's accusation: "You might have spared me a hundred pounds, Becky, out of all this—I have always shared with you" (chap. 53, p. 556).[23] And the last words he speaks in the novel are as ambiguous as any question from the narrator:

> "She has kep money concealed from me these ten years," he said. "She swore, last night only, she had none from Steyne. She knew it was all up, directly I found it. If she's not guilty, Pitt, she's as bad as guilty, and I'll never see her again, never."   (chap. 55, p. 579)

It is hardly possible to find the outrage of manly honor in these

[23] For a quite different interpretation, see Tillotson, *Novels of the Eighteen-Forties,* pp. 248, 251.

exactly struck last words. The distinction between "guilty" and "as bad as guilty" would be the final viciousness if it were not the final irrelevance.

But, again, is this what Thackeray means, and is it the *all* that he means? We can believe so only by acknowledging that the easy confidence between reader and writer promised at the beginning has been renounced, for we are here outside the domain of laziness, benevolence, or sarcasm. If the renunciation were the deliberate act of a supreme ironist who turns and rends us for our naive acceptance of his confidential detachment, Thackeray would indeed have created a masterpiece. But in the crucial scene and in portions of the chapters that lead to it Thackeray has exposed us to violent emotions that no politeness can conceal. The enmity between Little Rawdy and Lord Steyne, for example, is an extension of Becky's neglect of her child that erupts into physical violence: Becky boxes his ears for listening to her on the stairs as she entertains Lord Steyne (chap. 44, p. 460). The child indeed makes his first speaking appearance in the same chapter as that in which Lord Steyne also first appears, grinning "hideously, his little eyes leering towards Rebecca" (chap. 37, p. 389). The juxtaposition is emphasized when little Rawdon is apostrophized:

> O thou poor lonely little benighted boy! Mother is the name for God in the lips and hearts of little children; and here was one who was worshipping a stone.   (p. 392)

The appeal is no mere instance of competing with the creator of little Paul Dombey, as everyone who has read Thackeray's letters to his own mother will know. It is an appeal similar to many others in the narrative of Amelia, although there Thackeray is more characteristically reticent. When Amelia and her mother are reunited after her marriage, though Thackeray begins by referring to "How the floodgates were opened," he adds, "Let us respect Amelia and her mamma whispering and whimpering and laughing and crying in the parlour and the twilight." And when Amelia retreats to meditate in "the little room" with its "little white bed" in her old home, Thackeray desists:

> Have we a right to repeat or to overhear her prayers? These, brother, are secrets, and out of the domain of Vanity Fair, in which our story lies.   (chap. 26, pp. 262, 264)

Even—especially—if we construe this scene and its secrets as an expression of Amelia's first awareness that she is to be a mother herself, it still involves relationships and sentiments outside the "domain" that Thackeray so thoroughly explored. It is a domain bounded by the "politeness" invoked in that early address to the reader in which the narrator promises "to love and shake by the hand" his "good and kindly" characters, "to laugh confidentially in the reader's sleeve" at the "silly" ones, but "to abuse in the strongest terms that politeness admits of" all those who are "wicked and heartless" (chap. 8, p. 79). Such terms of abuse for the wicked and love for the good are for the most part so polite that we accept them with all the detachment guaranteed by the Manager of the Performance. But the limits of this detachment—its very bankruptcy—can be shown only as we glimpse the howling wilderness outside, where the secrets of private feelings are violently confused with public forces of huge and mysterious dimensions, and where there is neither lucidity nor truth.

What Thackeray does then exhibit within the domain of the Fair is the impossibility of self-knowledge and, in the fullest sense, dramatic change. The most intimate experiences of the self, whether in prayer or in love, in disappointment or in outrage, must be kept outside. Becky's "I am innocent" is no more an articulation of the truth than it is the lucid exposure of a lie. But to put us where we cannot know "What *had* happened" and to face us with the bewildering irrelevance of our polite detachment, Thackeray was driven to an extreme that no style of his could control. He could not be clear without being untruthful, and he could not be truthful without being obscure. He tried to recover himself, it is true, in the subsequent chapters by returning to the conception of Becky that most saves his book. The most interesting feature of her characterization is not that she begins from the ambiguous social position of the orphan and governess— " 'I don't trust them governesses, Pinner,' says the Sedley housekeeper with enormous assurance, 'they're neither one thing nor t'other. They give themselves the hairs and hupstarts of ladies, and their wages is no better than you nor me' " (chap. 6, p. 60). Thackeray is concerned with much more than the favorite Victorian example of social mobility. The greater truth about Becky is that she is a mimic, that she trades on the difference between fantasy and society, between the role and the fact. But the truth of endless mimicry is much too large for the domain of the lucid. It is larger than any drawing room, park, or square of Vanity Fair, and it could be forced in only by an act of violence that darkened lucidity and concealed truth. The casuistry upon which *Vanity Fair* rests is unique, and the responses of many thousands of readers for a hundred years to this much-read book must constitute one of the most erratic subterranean currents of our moral history.

Harold C. Martin

The Development of Style
in Nineteenth-Century American Fiction

Poetry, Mallarmé told Degas in an oft-quoted half-truth, is made with words—with words in order, he might have added; and prose, we infer, is made in the same way. If that is so, any sober analysis of style must be, in some measure, atomistic; it must separate components for examination even at the risk of temporarily losing sight of the whole. And an essay which pretends to examine the style of a century, even within one literary genre, can perhaps hope for little more than the elucidation of a few particulars. This essay, at least, attempts no more.

Because it casts its net so wide, this brief study needs, at the outset, some statement about the kind of fish it intends to catch. It is not a chronological study of style in American fiction. Nor is it the philosophical account of the "regular and contingent causes" of style for which William Wirt called in the tenth of his *Letters of the British Spy* (1832). It is, quite simply, no more than an attempt to distinguish and speculate about some significant changes in diction and in syntax—in words and in words-in-order—from the period in which American writers were either slavishly imitating the English or were consciously trying to be un-English to the period in which they had more or less successfully shaken themselves free of their literary inheritance and were developing traits of style for writers abroad to copy.

Two disadvantages are implicit in the procedure I have adopted: to set the limits at diction and syntax is to fall short of that synthesis which the critic hopes always to reach; and to attend only to those matters, without regard to plot, character, setting, or theme, is inevitably to magnify the peculiar merit of some authors and to slight the greater general merit of others. Both disadvantages may perhaps be forgiven as arising from the function of this essay as an introduction to a series on American fiction and as making possible the advantage of concreteness within a very wide compass.[1]

That there is a "development" in the style of prose fiction in nineteenth-century American literature no one is likely to dispute. And even a cursory acquaintance with that literature will lead any sensitive reader to conclusions about the development that are generally sound. It is worth while, nonetheless, to look at the evidence and to observe the course over which the noticeable changes have occurred.

Two narrative passages provide a text. The first is the opening paragraph of Stephen Crane's short story "The Open Boat," written in 1898. The other is from the fifth chapter of James Fenimore Cooper's fourth novel, *The Pilot,* written in 1823.[2] This is Crane:

[1] Except for casual mention, I have deliberately avoided discussion of Henry James's stylistic experiments and Mark Twain's more influential effort to accommodate colloquial style to prose fiction since separate papers in this series are devoted to those subjects.

[2] The text used here is that of the Author's Revised Edition, *The Works of*

None of them knew the color of the sky. Their eyes glanced level, and were fastened upon the waves that swept toward them. These waves were of the hue of slate, save for the tops, which were of foaming white, and all of the men knew the colors of the sea. The horizon narrowed and widened, and dipped and rose, and at all times its edge was jagged with waves that seemed to thrust up in points like rocks. Many a man ought to have a bath-tub larger than the boat which here rode upon the sea. These waves were most wrongfully and barbarously abrupt and tall, and each froth-top was a problem in small-boat navigation.

And here a somewhat similar scene penned seventy-five years earlier:

The rushing sounds of the wind were now, indeed, heard at hand; and the words were hardly past the lips of the young lieutenant, before the vessel bowed down heavily to one side, and then, as she began to move through the water, rose again majestically to her upright position, as if saluting, like a courteous champion, the powerful antagonist with which she was about to contend. Not another minute elapsed, before the ship was throwing the waters aside, with a lively progress, and, obedient to her helm, was brought as near to the desired course as the direction of the wind would allow. The hurry and bustle on the yards gradually subsided, and the men slowly descended to the deck, all straining their eyes to pierce the gloom in which they were enveloped, and some shaking their heads, in

---

J. Fenimore Cooper (New York, 1849–51). For this passage it is identical, except in minor matters of punctuation, with the text as originally published.

melancholy doubt, afraid to express the apprehensions they really entertained. All on board anxiously waited for the fury of the gale; for there were none so ignorant or inexperienced in that gallant frigate, as not to know that as yet they only felt the infant efforts of the wind. Each moment, however, it increased in power, though so gradual was the alteration, that the relieved mariners began to believe that all their gloomy forebodings were not to be realized. During this short interval of uncertainty, no other sounds were heard than the whistling of the breeze, as it passed quickly through the mass of rigging that belonged to the vessel, and the dashing of the spray that began to fly from her bows, like the foam of a cataract.

Now, Cooper's novel—though it is not entirely characteristic of the work with which he is today commonly identified—is in the strongest tradition of the period, that of the historical romance, modeled largely after Scott though influenced also by Fielding and Smollett. *The Pilot* is better than most of the romances published at the time; it is better, even, in some respects, than Cooper's later work; but it is close enough in particulars of style to contemporary works of the kind to provide a proper ground for generalization.

The most striking characteristic of this paragraph—for a modern reader, at least—is its syntax. The sentences are long: the first contains sixty-seven words; the last, fifty; the intermediate four average thirty-eight. All the sentences are complex or compound-complex, to use the grammarian's terms. All of the main clauses but one (the second in the third sentence) are clear of internal complication save for prepositional phrases.

That one is the second main clause of a compound-complex sentence; it incorporates, besides an early prepositional phrase, two parallel participial phrases, each of which in turn contains an infinitive phrase and a subordinate relative clause. Moreover, the simplicity of main clauses in the other five sentences is illusory, for the dependent clauses that follow each are as elaborately wrought as the main clause just described. Two have double predicates; all have internal adjectival or adverbial clauses; three have infinitive phrases, active or passive; and the last concludes with a relative clause, an infinitive, and five prepositional phrases, three of them final.

The sentences, we might say, unlike the ship, are heavily ballasted. They surge forward at the outset (only the last one has a phrase before the opening main clause), but they quickly develop complexity, yaw about, lose some of their momentum. That they do not lose more is the result of two things. Seven out of every ten words in the passage are monosyllabic. There are only five words of four syllables and two of five. The preponderance of monosyllables and the frequency of prepositional phrases produce a rising rhythm throughout. Considering the number of monosyllables it is worth noting that accented syllables come together only five times in the whole passage, twice to some semantic effect (*bowed down heavily, all straining*). Given the multiple iambic and anapestic feet and the few collisions of stress, the passage might indeed be unpleasantly undulant throughout if the substantive units, the combination of noun and modifier, did not generally provide emphasized clusters with falling rhythm (*rushing sounds, young lieutenant, upright position, courteous champion,* and so on).

In the felicity of his rhythms, as in the simplicity of opening clauses, Cooper is, in this novel, a better stylist than most of his contemporaries—Irving, of course, excepted. But the general structure of his sentences is also theirs. Even taken apart from vocabulary, this complex style indicates a deliberateness which removes action some distance from direct observation. Its lavish use of phrase and clause produces a syntactical separation of substantive and verb from modifier which reduces immediacy in perception. Its general leisureliness allows it to accommodate exposition and intermittent moralizing as well as narration without change in pace.

> Fancy, that stirring tormentor of acute minds, summoned up all his phantoms to Margaret's waking fears. . . .
>
> (John Pendleton Kennedy, *Horseshoe Robinson,* 1835)

> In all, indeed, there was the negative courtesy of that quiet and serious demeanor which solemn occasions impart to the rudest and most frivolous.
>
> (Beverly Tucker, *The Partisan Leader,* 1836)

In less able hands than Cooper's—those of William Gilmore Simms, for instance—the syntactical complications multiply and the prose becomes at times almost static regardless of the action or emotion involved. The impulse to decorate increases the paralysis, makes portraits out of descriptions and vignettes out of events. This, for example, is a moment of shocking discovery in Robert Bird's *Nick of the Woods,* (1837). Here the hero's party gets its first intimation of the presence of hostile Shawnees:

> Almost while he was yet speaking, the light, which all now

clearly beheld, at first a point as small and faint as the spark of a lampyris, and then a star scarce brighter or bigger than the touch of a jack o'lantern, suddenly grew in magnitude, projecting a long and lance-like, through broken, reflection over the wheeling current, and then as suddenly shot into a bright and ruddy blaze, illumining hill and river, and even the anxious countenances of the travellers.

Even in this technically loose sentence, the residual rhythms of a balanced prose can be discerned, and those rhythms are especially noticeable in the "set pieces," the descriptions of person and place, as well as in passages of recapitulation. It is clear that the convolutions of syntax in these romances is entirely consistent with the fictional method itself. The reader is being told, rather than shown, and the economy of telling— the arrangement of information by logical relations—is conventionally a generous one. If it provokes empathy, that is incidental; its purpose is to tell.

The vocabulary of Cooper's paragraph, we can tell without much study, is what we are accustomed to call a "literary" one. By that we generally mean non-colloquial, a vocabulary likely to contain more general and abstract than specific and concrete words, many words of Romance and Greek origin, a greater number of polysyllabic words than we customarily use in talking: in sum, a certain heaviness. In this particular passage, however, only one-sixth of the words have Latin roots, and several of that group have French correlates which are almost identical. The proportion is lower here than in most other novels of the kind, but not significantly so. The appearance of heaviness in this prose cannot fairly be ascribed, then, to etymology. Nor is it the result of excessive abstractness. Only sixteen words here,

I think, can qualify as abstract ones even by generous classification (*side, position, progress, direction, hurry, bustle, doubt, apprehension, fury, efforts, moment, power, alteration, forebodings, uncertainty, mass*); most of the nouns are concrete, though not specific. The historical romance actually forces concreteness on the author because it is committed to the recreation of the unfamiliar and thus to considerable pictorial exactitude. To the American romancer this was even more necessary than to his English counterpart: he wrote, more often than not, with an English audience in mind, but he wrote about a way of life completely unknown to them. The urge to be a realist, in this respect, is everywhere important in these early novels: objects of common utility in America are carefully described and their uses explained; words referring to common local customs are used, then paraphrased; dialect is translated (and often disparaged). Without the concreteness of these novels we would find them all but unreadable today, and even in their own time particularity of this kind must have been a welcome antidote to the prevailing sententiousness of authorial interpolations.

What I characterize as "heaviness" does, however, have some source in vocabulary as well as in syntax, and it derives from the relative insipidity of verbs. In the passage from *The Pilot,* a quarter of the words are nouns and pronouns, another quarter are adjectives and adverbs; only a tenth are verbs, and that tenth carry little weight or action. The verbs of the main clauses represent little more than states of being (*elapsed, subsided, waited, increased*) or action received (*were heard*); the strongest is *descended*. The verbs of action, many of them in the passive voice, appear only in subordinate clauses (*bowed, passed, be longed*), are frequently in the progressive or conditional tense (*was throwing, would allow*), or are compounded with infinitives (*began to move, was about to contend, began to believe, began to fly*). The most decisive action is harnessed into nouns and adjectives (*rushing sounds, powerful antagonist, lively progress, obedient to her helm, hurry, bustle, apprehensions, infant efforts*) or into participles and gerunds (*saluting, straining, shaking, whistling, dashing*). The total effect is to blunt action, to distribute the energy of action throughout the sentence, rather than to focus it for striking effect.

The same diffusion of energy is discernible in the variety of vocabulary. Six words of some importance are used twice (*wind, vessel, gradual*[*-ly*], *gloom*[*-y*], *power*[*-ful*], and *water*[*-s*]). Repetition is elsewhere avoided: *wind* is also *gale* and *breeze; vessel* is *ship* and *gallant frigate*. The economy is lavish, but some part of its fare we recognize, even at this distance, as hackneyed (*lively progress, to pierce the gloom, fury of the gale, gallant frigate, gloomy forebodings*), some part as circumlocutory (*afraid to express the apprehensions they really entertained*). This passage is relatively free, however, of catch-all intensifiers, so common to the type:

> Poor Arthur grew monstrous impatient in this gloomy abode.   (William Gilmore Simms, *Woodcraft*, 1852, 1854)

> The Piankeshaw, taking post directly in front of the hole, began to utter many mournful ejaculations, which were addressed to the insensate rock, or perhaps to the equally insensate corse of a comrade concealed within.
>
> (Bird, *Nick of the Woods*)

And it is reasonably free, as well, of the submission to stock locutions which is epidemic in these novels and, as a matter of fact, elsewhere in *The Pilot* and in others by Cooper, too:

> For a single instant, Birch was helpless, his blood curdling in his veins at the imminence of the danger, and his legs refusing their natural and necessary office.
>
> (Cooper, *The Spy,* 1821)

The point of such comment is not to belabor these novelists; it is clear that the stock epithets and the conventional phrasings are accepted as part of the decorum of the genre. Irving frequently complains about "cant," "jargon," the "hackneyed expression," yet his prose, too, abounds in phrases which have the ring of old silver, long in trade. The cause is not laziness—lazy authors do not write endless novels; nor is it indifference to the nature of rhetoric. It is, rather, another evidence of the "telling" relationship between author and reader, a relationship in which the reader is expected to be more passive than not.

Cooper's vigorous use of figurative language in this novel, as in *The Spy* but not in the Leatherstocking series, is unusual for the time in its persistence. Besides the continuous personification (*rushing sounds, winds would allow, hurry and bustle subsided, gloom in which they were enveloped, fury of the gale, powerful antagonist, infant efforts, whistling of the breeze, dashing of spray*) and the conventional similes (*like a courteous champion, like the foam of a cataract*), there is a thorough animation of the vessel itself: it *bowed, began to move, rose majestically . . . as if saluting, was about to contend, was throwing, was obedient*—it is a *gallant frigate.* Although such figurative intensity is rare in contemporary narration, the historical romances do find a place, and a large one, for figurative expression in the dialogue of their rustic characters. Indeed, they outdo each other in reproducing—or inventing—similes drawn from the experience of the uncultivated.

> He's a lazy, good for nuthin feller, Chil is. He's no better than a peaking mud-sucker. He lives on us all here like house-leek. He's no more use than yer prigged-up creepers. He is worse than the witches, vervain nor dill won't keep him away.
>
> (Sylvester Judd, *Margaret: A Tale of the Real and Ideal,* 1845)

> "Whar's your buffalo-bull," he cried, "to cross horns with the roarer of Salt River? Whar's your full-blood colt that can shake a saddle off? H'yar's an old nag can kick off the top of a buck-eye! Whar's your cat of the Knobs? your wolf of the Rolling Prairies? H'yar's the old brown b'ar can claw the bark of a gum-tree. . . . Ain't I a ring-tailed squealer? Can go down Salt on my back and swim up the Ohio! Whar's the man to fight Roaring Ralph Stackpole?"
>
> (Bird, *Nick of the Woods*)

But these extravagances, we must remember, are no part of the author's demeanor; they are the language of the unlettered, of what English novels using the same device refer to as "clowns." Beyond such use of figures for characterizing eccentricity, early novelists seldom venture. The novel-as-history and the novel-as-argument toward which these historical romances tend both promote discursiveness rather than concentration, and figurative language is not necessary to their purpose except in its more decorative forms.

Though more might be, enough has been said about the paragraph from Cooper's historical romance to give some idea of the vocabulary and syntax that govern the strongest and most serious tradition in the second quarter of the century and to underline the contrast between that tradition and the tradition represented in the opening paragraph from Crane's short story. This paragraph in a story some twelve or thirteen thousand words long contains, like the one from Cooper, six sentences, but those six sentences have fewer than half as many words. Although, in fact, only the first is a simple sentence, the complexity of none is great. There are nine main, or independent, clauses, and only four subordinate ones, and no subordinate clause contains any internal unit other than a prepositional phrase. One of the main clauses, on the other hand, has a double predicate, and another, a quadruple predicate. It is clear that the substance of action, then, is placed in a dominating position. This dominance is reinforced by successive rhythmic stresses at, or near, the opening of main clauses (*eyes glanced level, These waves* [repeated in the fifth sentence], *men knew, all times, each froth-top*). Moreover, the opening sentence is the shortest and sharpest of all: it is of nine words, all but one monosyllabic, and completely simple in syntax.

The change is a striking one, more striking than complete evidence for the period will bear out, yet correctly suggestive. It is not possible to trace the change in complete detail here, but I shall point out some of the way-stations. First, I want to make clear that the early part of the century is not without something like this compressed and forceful style, if not its precise parallel. The Augustan tradition of serried banks of balanced clauses frequently provides a succession of independent units, and it still finds occasional expression in three places: first, in the Addisonian "characters" developed in some historical romances (most notably in those of Simms and Kennedy) and in the hybrid essay-sketches of the Irving school; secondly, in passages of authorial criticism and lament, whatever the type of fiction; and, thirdly and rather curiously, in the novels of passion, where balanced clauses serve as restraints on the otherwise uninhibited excesses of declaration, protest, ecstasy, grief, and romantic despair. There is also a unique use of the short declarative sentence in the early novels of Charles Brockden Brown, a phenomenon worth noting since it seems to have caught Poe's attention; it is, at any rate, duplicated in some of his tales of the grotesque (most noticeably in "The Imp of the Perverse") and, shorn of subject-words and dried of its intensity, in the police reports of the tales of ratiocination, those forerunners of the detective story. A typical passage in Brown—there are literally scores of them, though the general progress of the novels uses a more complex syntax—is this, from an early page in *Wieland* (1798):

> I address no supplication to the Deity. The power that governs the course of human affairs has chosen its path. The decree that ascertained the condition of my life admits of no recall. No doubt it squares with the maxims of eternal equity. That is neither to be questioned nor denied by me. It suffices that the past is exempt from mutation.

By and large, however, the syntax of the whole period is

closer to that of Cooper, or even more relaxed. Washington Irving's is the master hand, and his informality, syntactically decorous though it is, reflects the very gradual enfranchisement from Augustan balances, parallels, and antitheses which the late eighteenth century achieved with such admirable success. What is peculiar to it, besides a general loosening from the Johnsonian or the Addisonian cadences, is the interpolation of the aside, the merely additive phrase, the grace note of intimacy:

> There is something nobly simple and pure in such a taste: it argues, I think, a sweet and generous nature, to have this strong relish for the beauties of vegetation, and this friendship for the hardy and glorious sons of the forest. There is a grandeur of thought connected with this part of the rural economy. It is, if I may be allowed the figure, the heroic line of husbandry.

> (Irving, *Bracebridge Hall*, 1822)

By means of these asides the author repeatedly pretends to disclaim the role of dogmatic philosopher. It is only a pretense, of course, for the authority he abandons in this regard he more than regains by the tone of intimacy. The stylistic effect of these interruptions is to produce a half-conversational rhythm, free of eccentricity and adaptable to various purposes. After Irving, Hawthorne's early tales and sketches reproduce it faithfully, sometimes when (as in "Rappaccini's Daughter" and in parts of the novels) it is not wholly felicitous. And the use of asides to break up the forward drive of syntax persists to the end of the century, becoming constantly more at odds, as in the novels of William Dean Howells, with the realistic tenor of late-century fiction.

The first sharp deviation from this Irvingesque graciousness is to be found, I think, in the work of John Neal, the Ezra Pound of early nineteenth-century criticism. Neal's assault on the dominant tradition concentrates its fire on exactly those stylistic conventions which had made Irving the universal model for the aspiring writer. Now Sterne's *Tristram Shandy* provided, of course, a ready model for any who chose to disrupt the elegance of orthodox syntax; but most Americans who admired Sterne's work, as a great many did, contented themselves with the creation of a whimsical character or two or with playful imitation of Sterne's diction:

> It is [Briggs says of the mint julep] . . . the homologous peculiar of the night,—the rectifier of the fancy,—the parent of pleasant dreams,—the handmaid of digestion, and the lullaby of the brain; in its nature essentially anti-roral; friendly to peristaltics and vermiculars; and in its influence upon the body, jocund and sedative.

> (John Pendleton Kennedy, *Swallow Barn,* 1832)

What Neal does is very different, and whether or not Sterne gave him the impetus is irrelevant. Neal's syntactical disjunctiveness is serious, not wayward or fanciful. He appears often to be attempting a representation of the intricacy of thought, as in this passage from *The Down-Easters* (1833):

> Well, the day passed over—and I received no sort of reply, not even a message, not a word nor a sign. Perhaps, thought I—perhaps it may be, for I heard her say once, I remember, that he was of a fiery quick temper, and very suspicious withal (I never thought of asking *why,* for although I

loved her as much as he loved her and might have been very sore with jealousy, *I* never suspected her faith, nor doubted her truth), it may be that she has written to me as she has, not on account of her love for me, but of her dread to him.

Or, in a less interesting but perhaps more influential deviation, he tries to develop syntactically the complication of sensory experience by the tumult of emotion:

He walked until he was tired—until he had lost himself. He stopped; and, immediately, there was a confused, eager whispering above him. He looked up. A scream followed. —He knew the voice, he could not be mistaken; though Arnold, he knew, did not live there. Edith might be out, on a visit. A female rushed by the row of large windows, overhead. He ran up the white marble steps to meet her— the door opened—ah! —It was a stranger! —No—not a stranger! —He staggered away. It was the beautiful creature, who had hunted him, so long; pursued him, like an evil spirit. He fled, with a cry of detestation; a look of hearty loathing; held on his way, through street, after street, until he was ready to drop; more than ever afraid of Edith, and of her purity; wondering why the bad apparition had overshadowed his path, at such a time; sick, weary, wretched, with a fear that he could not evade, nor overcome. His heart soon brought him to the right place. The moon was up; something familiar attracted his notice; and lifting his eyes, he saw the mansion of Arnold, before him.

(*Brother Jonathan*, 1825)

Once the breach in conventional syntax is made, other kinds of experimentation are inevitable. Melville's preoccupation with distinctive rhythmic movement provides a later example:

> At the same foam-fountain, Queequeg seemed to drink and reel with me. His dusky nostrils swelled apart; he showed his filed and pointed teeth. On and on we flew, and our offing gained, the Moss did homage to the blast; ducked and dived her bows as a slave before the Sultan. Sideways leaning, we sideways darted; every ropeyarn tingling like a wire; the two tall masts buckling like Indian canes in land tornadoes.   (*Moby-Dick*, 1851)

But the significant lines are those which Neal explores, never with enough care and never with complete success. His kind of starkness leads to Ambrose Bierce and on to Frank Norris, Robert Herrick, and Crane. His qualifying and requalifying prefigures Henry James and Edith Wharton. The aim, of course, is immediacy, a singleness of focus so intense that nothing extraneous to the dominant effect is allowed to intrude. The later concern for unity of impression may be largely the contribution of Poe, though he generally sought it by other means than the syntactical. But that syntax could be made to reinforce vocabulary in producing particular kinds of intensity seems to have occurred to Neal very early. In the century since Neal wrote his wild novels, the possibilities for such reinforcement have been exploited to the point of exhaustion. Crane's syntax stands about midway between the hasty experiments of Neal and the highly self-conscious syntactical experimentation of writers as diverse as Ernest Hemingway, William Faulkner, and Gertrude Stein.

The *language* of Crane's paragraph is as different from that of Cooper's as are their respective patterns of syntax. The number of monosyllables is slightly greater—eight of every ten words instead of seven—and the number of dissyllabic words commensurately smaller; but the passage contains only four longer words, less than a third the proportion in Cooper. What is of greater importance, the number of nouns and verbs increases as the number of adjectives and adverbs declines. The conjunctions, moreover, are overwhelmingly (three to one) coordinates. This dominance of substantives, verbs, and coordinating conjunctions, coupled with the syntactical characteristics already mentioned, indicates a localizing of action in the agent, rather than a distribution over the whole surface of the sentence. Further scrutiny of the verbs shows that even those cast in the passive voice and the copulas are here calculated to reinforce action, in this instance action on rather than by human beings.

The passage begins with a negative—*None of them knew the color of the sky*. The negative opening is strengthened in the next sentence by the second predicate: *Their eyes glanced level, and were fastened. . . .* From that point on the action is not that of the men but of their environment. The fifth sentence is generalized: *Many a man ought to have a bath-tub larger than the boat which here rode upon the sea.* It seems to me a failure, but its intent is surely to carry even further the annihilation of person begun in the first sentence.

More than half of the verbs themselves are indicative of strong action, a proportion less exclusive than later decades will require but much more absorptive than the early part of the century would admit; and, at the center of the passage, they take complete control: *The horizon narrowed and widened, and dipped and rose. . . .* The nouns, like those in Cooper's paragraph, are mainly concrete. Only eight of all the words, however, have roots of other than Saxon origin. It is interesting to note that four of these eight occur in the last sentence, the first two in conjunction with one of the rare trisyllabic words (*wrongfully and barbarously abrupt*), the other two (*problem, navigation*) in the rather unsuccessful closing predication. The first two call for attention because they are part of an effort to wrench words into new uses, an effort for which Crane was roundly criticized. The preceding sentence is of equal interest because of the word *bath-tub*. To begin with, the image is unexpected and incongruous; in 1898 it was indecorous as well. (Is it not the word that one of James's heroes never mentions as the source of his income?) Whether or not it is suitable here—I find it uncomfortably reminiscent of a common nursery rhyme—is for the moment unimportant. It serves my immediate purpose as an example of mixed diction.

There is, of course, an established tradition of mixed diction in American literature. Irving, for instance, often uses it for playful mockery:

> The villagers gathered in the church-yard to cheer the happy couple as they left the church; and the musical tailor had marshalled his band, and set up a hideous discord, as the blushing and smiling bride passed through a lane of honest peasantry to her carriage. The children shouted and threw up their hats; the bells rang a merry peal that set all the crows and rooks flying and cawing about the air, and threatened to bring down the battle-

ments of the old tower; and there was a continual popping off of rusty firelocks from every part of the neighborhood.

(Bracebridge Hall)

And Melville makes a particular virtue of mixture, melting jargon, dialect, elegant diction and low, apostrophe, rhapsody, and objurgation, in the same great pot. Twain and others use it for humor and pathos; the realists, for irony and sudden contrast.

But the use of *bath-tub* here, like the use of those two adverbs —*wrongfully* and *barbarously*—of a connotation particularly unusual in the context, is part of Crane's effort, and the effort of a few of his contemporaries, to rely on intensity of words rather than on variety and volume. In Crane, as in other writers of the period, realistic and romantic, the effort is accompanied by a preference for colloquial vocabulary. The result is a prose in which the possible variety has been deliberately limited, the number of repetitions therefore increased, and in which the use of striking words or images may be disproportionately frequent and, by virtue of the austere economy, particularly noticeable. The function of the author has changed from that of a "teller" to that of an "exciter"; he calculatedly provokes response in his readers by manipulating vocabulary.

Now it is obvious that there are more ways of exciting response than Crane attempts, and there is more than historical interest in examining some of them, for they, more than anything else, show the change in sensibility that comes over American fiction in the period with which I am concerned.

The early novels of romantic love, whose rigid syntax I earlier remarked, procure intensity by volume, even as they constantly protest the inadequacy of words to express their depth of feeling:

> Can time, can distance, can absence allay, or extinguish the sentiments of refined affection, the ardor of true love? No, my dear Eliza. If I may judge by my own heart, I shall say they cannot. Amidst the parade which has attended me, the interesting scenes in which I have been engaged, and the weighty cares, which have occupied my attention, your idea has been the solace of my retired moments; the soother of every anxious thought.
>
> (Hannah Webster Foster, *The Coquette or, the History of Eliza Wharton,* 1797)

This is a moderate epistle from an honorable lover; how much more extravagant is the language of false passion, I need not illustrate.

Brown's psychological novels use much the same method in what, to alter Henry James's observation slightly, is a terrible insistence of self-revelation:

> The petrifying influence of surprise yielded to the impetuosities of passion. I held him in my arms; I wept upon his bosom; I sobbed with emotion which, had it not found passage at my eyes, would have burst my heartstrings.   (*Edgar Huntley,* 1799)

Another kind of voluminousness, one which finds an echo in the realistic fiction of the nineties, seeks not so much an intensity of feeling as an intensity of scene or of action. The device is one of cataloguing, of adding item to item until sheer detail produces the impression sought.

Entering the store you beheld a motley array of dry and

fancy goods, crockery, hardware, and groceries, drugs and medicines. On the right were rolls of kerseymeres, callimancoes, thicksets, durants, fustians, shaloons, antiloons, ratteens, duffils and serges of all colors; Manchester checks, purple and blue calicoes; silks, ribbons, oznaburgs, ticklenbergs, buckram. On the left were cuttoes, Barlow knives, iron candlesticks, jewsharps, blackball, bladders of snuff; in the left corner. . . .   (Sylvester Judd, *Margaret*)

This sort of thing, handled with more imagination, is common in Melville and almost a stock-in-trade of the realist:

The labourers went trudging past in a straggling file—plumbers' apprentices, their pockets stuffed with sections of lead pipe, tweezers, and pliers; carpenters, carrying nothing but their little pasteboard lunch baskets painted to imitate leather; gangs of street workers, their overalls soiled with yellow clay, their picks and long-handled shovels over their shoulders; plasterers, spotted with lime from head to foot. This little army of workers, tramping steadily in one direction, met and mingled with other toilers of a different description—conductors and "swing men" of the cable company going on duty; heavy-eyed night clerks from the drug stores on their way home to sleep; roundsmen returning to the precinct police station to make their night report, and Chinese market gardeners teetering past under their heavy baskets.   (Frank Norris, *McTeague,* 1899)

However adroitly managed, intensity produced by volume eventually vitiates interest unless something more than the denotative content of the words is exploited. The work of exploring other sources of intensity in words is intimately connected with the development of that half-chimerical phenomenon, transcendentalism, which affected American life and letters so variously for more than fifty years. A feeling grows that words may, like the rope-ladder of Father Mapple's pulpit, "symbolize something unseen," as Hester's scarlet "A," thrown from her breast and floating on the brook, becomes an impassable barrier between her and the inscrutable daughter of her sin. The anagogical relations between earth and infinity which preoccupy Judd's heroine in *Margaret* are implicit throughout Melville, even in the chapter headings (The Nut, The Fountain, The Tail, The Try-Works, The Lamp), the particular expanding endlessly to the universal. In Poe exploitation of the word is almost obsessive, but it takes a different turn; not simply the reference, but the sound, the location of stress, the "color" of the word are all treated as if pregnant with meaning. Indeed, these latter are often more important than reference. Poe's vocabulary is not so much precise as vivid and euphonious. The House of Usher is surrounded by a "black and lurid tarn that lay in unruffled lustre by the dwelling," a collocation of Poe's favorite colors which surely requires some suspension of disbelief. Poe's preoccupation with the mirror-image (in "William Wilson," 1840, and elsewhere), with the mystery behind the superficial exactness of reflection, leads him to press word upon word, phrase upon phrase, as though the essence of each were ineffable and the possibility of truth lay only in probing many, however incongruous the combination:

> His voice [the narrator says of Roderick Usher] varied rapidly from a tremulous indecision (when the animal spirits seemed utterly in abeyance) to that species of energetic concision—that abrupt, weighty, unhurried, and hollow-

sounding—that leaden, self-balanced and perfectly modulated guttural utterance, which may be observed in the lost drunkard, or the irreclaimable eater of opium, during the periods of his most intense excitement.

("Fall of the House of Usher," 1839)

One has the sense, to use Poe's own words, of being "upon the very verge of remembrance" ("Ligeia" and "Murders in the Rue Morgue": "upon the brink of . . ."), or on the point of discovery, but never in full possession of it.

Although no other important writers in the century, so far as I know, follow Poe in this attempt to extort intensity from words by such perfervid insistence on the use of all their properties, there is, surely, something of the kind in James as there is, later, in Faulkner. Poe's concern for *unity of impression,* however, is undoubtedly influential not only on the structure of all later fiction but on its vocabulary as well.

That concern is, of course, always in some measure in an author's mind and proceeds almost automatically from the skilled writer, whatever his subject and whatever his tone. It is a chief charm of Irving's style, for instance, that his voice is everywhere heard through his matter. But Poe's idea of unity precludes the author's presence; the unity must be that of the matter alone, a total concentration on the event. For such concentration he usually employs an alliterative compound of vivid and suggestive words:

> The senses were oppressed by mingled and conflicting perfumes, reeking up from strange convolute censers, together with multitudinous flarings and flickering tongues of emerald and violet fire.   ("The Assignation," 1835)

But the language need not be of this kind. It may be entirely blunt, stripped of superficially evocative associations, and still send down depth-charges. The concern is not for the *mot juste* but for the *mot resonant*.

Various influences in the post-war period shift emphasis away from Poe's declared method. Foremost among them are a resistance to the inherent vagueness of transcendental writing, the enduring strength of the tradition of local color, and the strong emotional impact of the bloody war and of the feverish economic and industrial growth that followed it. The fiction of that period less and less retains the flavor of literary culture, even in the work of curious and cultivated men like Henry Adams. Latin, French, and German tags disappear. (Simms could, without noticeable absurdity, describe the appearance of a frontiersman as *outré*.) More or less gratuitous allusions to classical lore disappear with them. (Half of the hardies in early historical romances are, at one time or another, referred to as Briareus.) The tropes come now, as they formerly did only in the dialogue of rustics, from the immediate experience of the characters ("a knotty hand like a bunch of prison keys" —Bierce; sunbeams "like a powerful search-light"—Harte; the Board of Trade building like "the maw of some colossal sewer"—Norris). For long stretches there may be no overt figures at all but a steady undercurrent of working metaphors into which action and supplementary meaning are packed together. The early and awkward attempts to approximate uncultivated speech over which pre-war writers labored so self-consciously become steadily less constrained, less affected; the idiom of farm, mining town, and city tenement creeps over into narration and description.

Naturally, this does not happen all at once, and it does not happen uniformly. But it affects even the more conservative writers. (The italics in all examples are mine.)

Joseph Twombly, ex-knight and capitalist, had bowed gracefully and good-humoredly to fate, instead of throwing up his hands and rending his garments, *like other people we know of.* (Thomas Bailey Aldrich, *Prudence Palfrey,* 1874)

Bartley felt like resenting the freedom, but he was anxious *to pour his ideas* of journalism into the manager's sympathetic ear, and he began to talk, with an impression that it behooved him *to talk fast.*

(William Dean Howells, *A Modern Instance,* 1882)

Meanwhile Doris was growing more and more pleased with the day's enterprise. To be sure, there were clouds in the sky, but they afforded a subject for discussion rather than alarm, and *the weather suited exactly.*

(Sarah Orne Jewett, *A Marsh Island,* 1885)

She was waked by the news that in the night her father had been seized by another paroxysm, and that although better, he was excessively weak. He had forbidden his attendants to call her, on the cool calculation that *he would probably pull through this attack,* and that she would need all her strength for the next.

(Henry Adams, *Esther,* 1884)

Among those writers more determined to concentrate effect, the change consists not only in adapting to all purposes the

relatively bare language of the colloquial but also in deliberate
spareness, in repeated use of a key word, in the shock of unexpected, though apposite, metaphor:

> . . . [McTeague] was too hopelessly stupid to get much
> benefit from [books] (p. 2). Altogether he suggested the
> draught horse, immensely strong, stupid, docile, obedient
> (p. 3). Absolutely stupid, and understanding never a word,
> McTeague would answer . . . (p. 19).
>
> (Frank Norris, *McTeague*)

The youth desired to screech out his grief. He was stabbed,
but his tongue lay dead in the tomb of his mouth.

> (Crane, *The Red Badge of Courage*, 1895)

The expressionistic intensity of Poe is replaced by an impressionism equally intense and more startling:

The red sun was pasted in the sky like a wafer.

> (Crane, *The Red Badge of Courage*)

The economy is a new one because the role of the author
has changed. The vocabulary is new because the range of
subject matter and the sensibilities of writer and reader alike
have changed. Syntax has come closer to the patterns of normal
conversation or has been stylized into something even more
abrupt and free of logical connectives. The leisurely decorum
of earlier novels has been replaced by what George Washington
Cable called "this gratuitous Yankee way of going straight to
the root of things."

Whether or not this considerable change argues a like alteration of any depth in the writers, it is harder to say. Human
nature does not, one would think, change greatly in a hundred

years; but modes of thinking do, and it may for that reason be wise to end not with Buffon's familiar dictum about style and the man but with Remy de Gourmont's refinement of his fellow countryman's aphorism:

Le signe de l'homme dans l'oeuvre intellectuelle, c'est la pensée. La pensée est l'homme même. Le style est la pensée même.

John C. Gerber

The Relation between Point of View
and Style in the Works of Mark Twain

Possibly William Dean Howells best got at the heart of what critics and scholars have had to say about Mark Twain's work when he wrote that Twain's

> great charm is absolute freedom in a region where most of us are fettered and shackled by immemorial convention. He saunters out into the trim world of letters, and lounges across its neatly kept paths, and walks about on the grass at will, in spite of all the signs that have been put up from the beginning of literature, warning people of dangers and penalties for the slightest trespass.[1]

Brander Matthews gave this point a more specific turn with respect to style: "He imparted to the printed page the vivacity of the spoken word, its swiftness and its apparently unpremeditated ease."[2] And Bernard DeVoto became more specific still when he celebrated Twain's style for its simplicity, its adaptability, its intimate liaison with the senses, and its fidelity to the idioms of speech.[3] An apparently unmanipulated colloquialism

[1] *My Mark Twain* (New York, 1910).
[2] *Essays on English* (New York, 1921), p. 248.
[3] *Mark Twain's America* (Boston, 1932), p. 318.

—what the *Times Literary Supplement* calls "an inspired casualness and realism" [4]—this seems by general agreement to be the chief hallmark of Twain's style.

But this is not to say that Twain's style is all of a piece. Like talk itself, it runs the full gamut from the brilliant to the inane. Bret Harte noticed this range as early as 1870 when in reviewing *Innocents Abroad* he called attention not only to Twain's vigorous rhetoric and original humor, but also to his sentimentality in diction, his clichés, and his journalistic flourishes. [5] Walter Blair probably speaks for most contemporary readers when he writes that Twain's stylistic sins are many and that his greatness is not to be found in works as wholes but in passages within those works, especially passages in *The Gilded Age, Tom Sawyer, Huckleberry Finn, Pudd'nhead Wilson, Life on the Mississippi,* and *Tom Sawyer Abroad.* [6]

What I should like to do here is not to reaffirm or even elaborate upon such commonly accepted opinions as these, but rather to get behind them and try to account for the erratic stylistic achievement which they suggest. More particularly I should like to argue that Twain's style is so intimately dependent upon his point of view that it flourishes only to the extent that the point of view is detached and sharply restricted. A detached point of view, by providing him with psychological distance, results in a better controlled and more consistent style. A sharply restricted point of view, by forcing him to focus upon a specific and concrete situation, results in a more sensitive and pictorial style. A

---

[4] September 17, 1954, p. xii.

[5] *Overland Monthly,* Vol. IV o.s. (January, 1870), in *Mark Twain: Selected Criticism,* ed. by Arthur L. Scott (Dallas, Texas, 1955), pp. 13–16.

[6] *Native American Humor* (New York, 1937), p. 159.

combination of the two results in the finest efforts of his imagination. On the other hand, a vague and highly personal viewpoint seems not only to allow but to encourage Twain to give expression to his personal opinions, prejudices, disharmonies, irrelevancies, whimsies, and contradictions at the expense of the subject matter and to the detriment of the style. The writing may be colorful in such instances, but it calls attention to itself and in the end is ineffective.

I am not arguing, of course, that point of view is the *only* force that shapes Twain's style. There are obviously many others. But I *am* contending that it is a major force. The evidence for this contention, it seems to me, can be found in all his more important works, though in this paper I shall consider only seven.

I

Until 1869, when he published *Innocents Abroad,* Twain brought out only one piece that is still widely read, "The Jumping Frog of Calaveras County." It seems no coincidence that this is the only substantial piece in this period in which the points of view are both detached and sharply restricted. As narrator of the frame element Twain plays the part of an elegant, educated, solemn ass who can't see anything out of the way even in searching for a minister in Angel's Camp. As Simon Wheeler, narrator of the inner element, he plays the role of an equally solemn character, but this time one who is uneducated. Both roles were well known to Twain. The first he had seen played by Artemus Ward in his Virginia City lectures.[7] The second he knew from experience with a long line of garrulous old codgers from his own Uncle John Quarles of Florida, Missouri, to Ben Coon of Calaveras County, from whom Twain says he got the frog story itself. Furthermore, he had seen the same combination of narrators used effectively in the works of such Southwestern yarnspinners as T. B. Thorpe and George W. Harris. The result is a happy consistency in the style of each narrator and an engaging contrast between the two styles.

Both narrators give the impression of addressing the reader directly—one assuming that he is a reader and the other that he is a listener—but there the likeness ends. The narrator of the frame story is literary, formal, and dull. He even indulges in such expressions as "and I hereunto append the result." Simon Wheeler, on the other hand, speaks in the vernacular. And in his long drawling sentences we encounter for the first time that deceptive casualness of Twain's. Seemingly Wheeler is simply rattling on about the infamous Jim Smiley, giving details as they occur to him. Actually his speech is carefully manipulated for the purpose of climax, and the style supports this arrangement. As the story proceeds the diction becomes more colorful and the figures of speech more numerous and more picturesque. Increasingly one gets the sense not only of the fact of the experience but of its especial quality, witness the frog in the last third of the account as it "snakes" a fly off

[7] In this connection it should be remembered that "The Jumping Frog" first came out as a letter to Ward. The letter form was inconsequential and was later dropped, but thinking about the story originally as a letter to Ward must have influenced Twain in his selection of narrators.

the counter, flops on the floor again "as solid as a gob of mud," and falls to "scratching the side of his head with his hind foot as indifferent as if he hadn't no idea he'd been doin' any more'n any frog might do." Dialogue, moreover, is introduced in this last third, the shorter rhythms of Jim Smiley and the stranger breaking into and keeping Wheeler's longer rhythms from becoming tedious. Colorful and imaginative, though not grotesquely so, Simon Wheeler's talk is one of Twain's finest stylistic achievements.

In the seven years after "The Jumping Frog" Twain busied himself primarily with travel writing: twenty-five letters to the Sacramento *Union* about his experiences in the Sandwich Islands, twenty-six letters to the *Alta California* about his trip across the Nicaraguan Penninsula and back east, fifty-three letters to the *Alta* plus a few to the New York *Tribune* and the *Herald* about his trip to the Holy Land, and finally two books based in part on these letters, *Innocents Abroad* (1869) and *Roughing It* (1872). Since the relation between point of view and style is substantially the same in all of these works—and in subsequent travel books also—I shall confine this discussion to the first of the books, *Innocents Abroad*.

Twain's point of view in *Innocents* is fundamentally that of the letter writer, and the style reflects the letter writer's sense of intimacy with his reader. Twain refers to himself as "I," to his party as "we," and occasionally to the reader as "you." The sentences are primarily simple or compound; the diction is familiar; the comparisons, both literal and figurative, are taken from everyday life; and there is an astonishing profusion of questions and exclamations. Such, at least, is one's first impression. Actually, however, the situation is not nearly so simple. The point of view of the letter writer is a loose, ill-defined one that imposes few restrictions and almost no psychological distance upon Twain. On the contrary, it allows him within its generous confines to do a variety of things or, if you will, play a variety of roles, changing his cap as the spirit moves him. On occasion, for example, he is simply the purveyor of information; at other times he is the on-the-spot observer, the satirist, the humorous raconteur, and the amiable idiot. Since each of these roles varies in its demands, each exerts its own special pressure upon the style. The result is an almost wild profusion of styles despite the basic colloquialism.

As a purveyor of information Twain is easily at his dullest. Aping the stolid, unimaginative approach of the typical guidebook writer, he delivers himself of his facts with the same flatness. Even worse, he uses the same clichés and absurd rhetorical flourishes. We are treated, for instance, to short accounts of the "stalwart Bedouins of the desert" and the "stately Moors, proud of a history that goes back to the night of time." Venetian fleets, we learn, used to bring back "products of every clime," and one portion of Notre Dame Cathedral is "suggestive of the quaint fashions of ancient times." To Twain's credit, however, it should be said that he does occasionally try to spice up his guidebook style with colloquialisms and homely contrasts. Thus, though the Temple of Jupiter at Baalbec is "a wonder of architectural beauty and grandeur," the blocks used in its construction are about as long as "three street cars."

When Twain assumes the role of on-the-spot observer he employs a sharper focus, and his style livens up. The results

can best be seen in the colorful descriptions of such places as
Flores, Tangiers, and Lake Como. Even in these, however,
the focus is still not so sharp as it might be, for there is a
strong tendency to view the material in the conventional, two-
dimensional way. In less noteworthy passages the wording is
frequently too general (the water of the Blue Grotto is described as "ravishing" and "superb"); often the figures of speech
are incongruous (from the eaves to the comb of the roof the
curved marble beams of Milan cathedral stretch "like the fore-
and-aft braces of a steamboat"); and sometimes the diction
is almost appalling (the catacombs of the Capuchin Convent are
"upholstered" by the bones of four thousand monks).

Twain never remains the on-the-spot observer very long without slipping into the role of satirist. This is the role that
affords him the least detachment of any. For Twain is too
emotional, too contradictory in his thinking to be able to work
as a satirist should in a controlled manner from firm premises.
As a result he protests too much, as though the police siren were
a substitute for the rapier. His words become overcharged with
feeling, his details are exaggerated, he resorts repeatedly to the
silliest kind of parody and the most obvious kind of sarcasm and
invective; and over all there is a general straining for effect
that calls attention to itself instead of to the subject matter. In
Italy, for example, he cannot restrain his sarcasm in writing about
the "dead and damned Medicis" who, as he says, "had their
trivial, forgotten exploits on land and sea pictured out in grand
frescoes . . . with the Saviour and the Virgin throwing bouquets
to them out of the clouds, and the Deity himself applauding from
his throne in Heaven!" Bored and irritated by the Mosque of

Santa Sophia, he describes it as the "rustiest barn in heathendom" and claims that he got so stuck up in it on "a complication of gums, slime, and general corruption" that he wore out two thousand bootjacks getting his shoes off that night. In Galilee he becomes exasperated with the indifference of adults to the health of their children, and slaps out these almost nauseating images:

> Yesterday we met a woman riding on a little jackass, and she had a little child in her arms; honestly, I thought the child had goggles on as we approached, and I wondered how its mother could afford so much style. But when we drew near, we saw that the goggles were nothing but a camp meeting of flies assembled around each of the child's eyes, and at the same time there was a detachment prospecting its nose. (Vol. II, chap. 18)

Twain himself once said that he could never be a good satirist because he felt too deeply. There is much truth in the remark.

When Twain shifts from satire to humorous storytelling, his style undergoes an almost dramatic change as the result of the narrower focus and the increased detachment that the role of raconteur affords him. The details are more specific and the incidents far better shaped for climax. Many of the stories are adaptations of old anecdotes, but the best are from his own experience: making a fool of the Genoese guide, taking a Turkish bath, and betting an Arab he can't go from the top of the pyramid of Cheops to the top of the pyramid of Cephron and back again in nine minutes. When his role as storyteller offers him sufficient psychological distance he even slips into understatement. Here is the climax of the story in which he claims as a boy to have seen a corpse by the moonlight in his father's office.

> I went away from there. I do not say that I went away in any sort of hurry, but I simply went—that is sufficient. I went out of the window, and I carried the sash along with me. I did not need the sash, but it was handier to take it than it was to leave it, and so I took it. I was not scared, but I was considerably agitated. (Vol. I, chap. 18)

The simplicity of these sentences and words—most of the words are monosyllables—is worth comparing with the gaudy rhetoric so characteristic of the satirical passages. Incidentally, the fact that this quietly effective style occurs in a passage where Twain is temporarily assuming the point of view of a boy should not be overlooked.

The role of the amiable idiot is the most restricted one that Twain plays in *Innocents Abroad*. As the idiot Twain pretends to believe everything that is told him, no matter how preposterous. More than that, he displays anxiety that the reader believe it too. The result is an earnest, solemn, and still effective style quite in conflict with the silly evidence and absurd logic.

It may be contended that Twain is not playing different roles in *Innocents Abroad* but simply changing his attitude and techniques with the material. There is something to such a contention since the material to a certain extent does affect Twain's personal involvement, scenery for example tending to leave him relatively detached and the sight of human depravity tending to engage his strongest emotions. But this is not the whole story, for he views the same kind of material in different ways. And besides, certain of the roles Twain plays are impossible to conceive of as merely moods or shifts in attitude. No author can be as shrewd as Twain is in some passages and then as incredibly stupid as he is in others unless he is shifting his role as narrator.

2

From 1873 to 1884 Twain's most important works dealt in part or in whole with the Mississippi valley: *The Gilded Age* (1873), "Old Times on the Mississippi" (1875; later enlarged into *Life on the Mississippi,* 1883), *Tom Sawyer* (1876), and *Huckleberry Finn* (1885). Taken in chronological order these works offer a four-step progression toward the detached and sharply restricted point of view of the boy, the point of view that results in Twain's most brilliant stylistic achievement.

In those parts of *The Gilded Age* which he wrote, Twain gains detachment by shifting to the viewpoint of the omniscient author. And in the several passages where he carefully restricts his focus, the writing is comparable with his best.

Not all of the effects of third-person narration are helpful to the style. Rather clearly Twain in the opening chapter is fighting the distance enforced by this point of view, for he tries to retain the colloquial intimacy of first-person writing by referring to the reader as "you" and to himself as "we." Apparently, however, he soon discovers the awkwardness of this effort and drops the attempt. In its place he adopts a bizarre informality achieved by italics, exclamations, asides to the reader in brackets, soliloquies addressed by characters to the reader, dialogue set up in play form, and even a discussion with the reader over the merits of two possible denouements. The shift to the third person also brings him more clearly under the influence of the sentimental novelists. Like them he begins referring to his readers as "our readers" and to a character as "our hero." And some of his scenes for what Huck calls "tears and flapdoodle" would do credit to Mrs. E. D. E. N. Southworth herself.

Yet on the whole the style of Twain's portions of *The Gilded Age* is superior to that of his travel books. For one thing it is more consistent. The sudden jumps from expository to satirical to narrative writing and back again are neither so frequent nor so jarring. For another, the satiric effects are better shaped and sustained. To be sure, the satire is still flamboyant—maybe more so than before—and the same devices are exploited. But with Twain not so much in evidence and his personal feelings not so much a topic of discussion, the thrust of the satire is less diffuse. There is nothing in the travel books, it seems to me, so devastating as the trial of Laura Hawkins, the repudiation by the Senate of Senator Noble, or even the speech by that arch-scoundrel, Senator Dilworthy, before the Sunday School of Cattleville.

Twain's greatest stylistic achievement in *The Gilded Age,* however, is the talk of Colonel Beriah Sellers. For the purpose of this argument it is important to notice that Colonel Sellers's best talk is in the early Hawkeye scenes where his listener is the youthful Washington Hawkins, and that in these scenes Twain as omniscient author has moved into the mind of Hawkins. At best this is no more than a tentative step toward surrendering to the sharply restricted viewpoint of the boy, but even this tentative step produces brilliant results.

In the seven pieces sent to Howells for the *Atlantic* in 1875 and entitled "Old Times on the Mississippi" Twain returns to first-person narration, but under circumstances that are much more auspicious than those that prevailed in the travel accounts. His function as narrator in the *Atlantic* pieces is obviously clearer to him and more restricted: he is the raconteur reminiscing about his days of piloting. The lapse of time since his pilot days provides a distance he does not ordinarily have in the travel works, and the material is familiar and close to his heart. It is not surprising, therefore, that in over-all quality "Old Times" is far better than the travel works. Indeed, some passages are among his best stylistic efforts, especially those in which Twain identifies himself with and partly submits to the limitations of a boy's point of view.

This partial submission is apparent first in the opening chapter entitled "A Boy's Ambition," in which Twain tells of the Hannibal of his youth, of the contrast between the town as it usually was and the town when a steamer arrived. It also occurs in the passages dealing with the adventures of the cub pilot. In these Twain is presumably writing about himself, but, as many have observed, the cub pilot of "Old Times" is a far younger and greener youth than Twain would have been. Actually Twain was close to twenty-two when he asked Horace Bixby to "learn" him the river. He was probably as sophisticated about the river and river boats as any neophyte pilot ever was. But the cub pilot of "Old Times" is so naive he doesn't know he has to stand a regular watch, he is ignorant about fast and slow water, and he thinks Bixby points out landmarks just to be sociable. Lively and curious, he is nevertheless the veriest of greenhorns and cannot plausibly be more than sixteen, if he is even that.

What Twain does in each of these passages is to begin with his own point of view as author; then he moves into the boy's mind, reporting what he sees and hears, his reactions, and occasionally his motives; and finally he returns to the authorial point of view as the incident or passage comes to an end. As a matter of fact, his attempt to recover the boy's point of view is even more substantial than this account suggests, for in narrating each adventure he confines himself largely to the stuff of experience that would attract the boy. The adult commentary he saves for the transitional passages or for separate chapters.

The style of the narrative passages is fresh and pictorial, with the rhythms adapted to the tension of the incident. This is true not only of the parts (such as the sharp concrete detailing, the use of technical river terms, and the rendering of river talk) but also of the over-all effect, which suggests at once the wonder, the humor, and the dangers of piloting. Some of this writing achieves an extraordinary vividness and economy.

> Behind other islands we found wretched little farms, and wretcheder little log-cabins; there were crazy rail fences sticking a foot or two above the water, with one or two jeans-clad, chills-racked, yellow-faced male miserables roosting on the top-rail, elbows on knees, jaws in hand, grinding tobacco and discharging the results at floating chips through crevices left by lost teeth; while the rest of the family and

the few farm animals were huddled together in an empty wood-flat riding at her moorings close at hand. (chap. 11)

Those sections of "Old Times" written from the grown-up's point of view, while chatty, are much less vigorously executed. Even so, they are stylistically superior to most of the chapters added in 1883 to make up *Life on the Mississippi*. In these later portions, largely the result of a trip back to the Mississippi in 1882, we are right back among the travel books. Again writing in the first person without any basic restriction, Twain changes his style with his purpose or pose of the moment. The writing is at its best when he has somebody else tell a story, as in Huck's account of the visit to the raft or the "handsome man's" account of the Darnell-Watson feud. It is at its worst in the dreary historical and geographical disquisitions at the beginning and the guide-book writing at the end. Indeed this latter apparently gets so tedious even for Twain that he calls on an old gentleman who gets on board at LaCrosse to continue the account by delivering a travelogue plagiarized from a railroad advertising folder. Then Twain shamelessly ridicules the folder's style, though its fancy rhetoric is no worse than what he himself has been using. Even a set description of the Mississippi, as Leo Marx has pointed out,[8] is little more than a "pretty picture" described in soft, conventional terms. It is not the Mississippi itself, therefore, that seems to stir Twain's genius. It is the Mississippi seen with the fresh, detached, finely focused vision of a boy.

[8] "The Pilot and the Passenger: Landscape Conventions and the Style of *Huckleberry Finn*," *American Literature*, XXVIII (May, 1956), 129–46. I am indebted also to this article for subsequent remarks on landscape description in *Tom Sawyer* and *Huckleberry Finn*.

In *Tom Sawyer* Twain takes another step toward such a viewpoint. To be sure, he continues to write as the grown-up. But the grown-up point of view in *Tom Sawyer* is much less of a controlling force than it is in "Old Times." Partly this is because the shift to third-person narration makes it more implicit than explicit. More fundamentally, however, it is because Twain becomes more interested in Tom than he ever was in his cub pilot, and hence more eager to explore Tom's point of view. In effect, he partly surrenders himself to Tom or (to extend T. S. Eliot's notion of Twain as a combination of Tom and Huck) to the Tom in himself. What we have in *Tom Sawyer*, then, is a reasonably stable blend throughout the book of the two points of view, the adult's and the boy's. The style is clearly the product of this blend.

Much of the writing suggests that Twain is conscientiously attempting to realize the boy's vitality and directness, his careful observation, his imagination and love of display. Evidence for this intention can be found particularly in the much higher proportion of concrete material than we have seen before—and not only in the proportion of such material but in its quality as well. The details, taken as a whole, are more sharply observed, and the scenes begin to assume a third dimension. Perhaps one can see the influence of Tom's point of view, also, in the increasing interest in dialogue and in the constant manipulation of material for climax or "effects." Certainly, it seems to me, one can see it in the sentences, which have a livelier forward propulsion achieved by increased simplicity, by the brevity of the transitions, and by an emphasis almost like a beat on the main verbs.

But there is much in the style of *Tom Sawyer* that still reflects the grown-up. It is the adult mind that is responsible for words like *cogitate, pariah, fillup,* and *hypercritical,* for generalizations about the boys, for tags like "these curiously inconsistent pirates," and for the fun poked at the girls' compositions. It is Twain, the grown-up author, too, who is responsible for the continuing tendency to see phenomena in terms of clichés ("eaten up with envy," "perennial bliss"), to personify nature ("the marvel of Nature shaking off sleep and going to work unfolded itself to the musing boy"), and to sentimentalize (see almost any scene involving Aunt Polly). Finally, and more to its credit, it is the grown-up point of view that is responsible for the gentle and amiable irony which suffuses the book and gives it its dominant tone.

When he first saw the manuscript of *Tom Sawyer* Howells wrote to Twain, advising him to treat the book explicitly as a boy's story. "Grown-ups," he said, "will enjoy it just as much if you do; and if you should put it forth as a study of boy character from the grown-up point of view, you give the wrong key to it." [9] Mrs. Clemens agreed with Howells, and of course so did Twain. As a result, Twain toned down a satirical passage or two and lopped off what he had meant to be the last chapter. But the advice came too late to affect the book fundamentally. And so it remains only a partial attempt to catch the boy's point of view. The full attempt comes in the book he started immediately after completing *Tom Sawyer* but did not complete until eight years later: *Huckleberry Finn.*

[9] *Mark Twain's Letters,* ed. by Albert B. Paine (New York, 1917), I, 266.

3

The most significant decision Mark Twain makes in beginning to write *Huckleberry Finn* is to have Huck tell the story. By this one decision he provides himself with a point of view that offers both the curbs and the detachment that his imagination needs for its best efforts. Almost magically it discourages him from doing the things he does badly and encourages him to do the things he does best. What is most important is not simply that Huck is a boy, though that is important; it is the kind of boy that Huck is.

Huck is a serious boy. From the very first, Twain makes him the straight, almost solemn reporter, with little or no sense of humor. Fog on the river, Pap's drunkenness, Miss Watson's piety, and the Royal Nonesuch, these are all solemn facts of life to Huck, no one of them to be regarded as less serious or more trivial than another. His own statements he takes as equally solemn facts, no matter how ludicrous they may be to the reader. He can report with sober admiration that Uncle Silas Phelps "never charged nothing for his preaching, and it was worth it too." This is the poker-face style elevated and made sincere.

Having created such a character as narrator, Twain can hardly use him for his usual plunges into Washoe-type humor. Huck, who in a sense becomes stronger than Twain, won't be a party to such foolishness, though he is willing to report it as he hears it from others. So Twain is forced either to tone down his exaggerations and burlesques or to parcel them out to other characters. He does both, and in either case they get toned down, because in parceling them out he causes them to become revelations of character as well as means of evoking laughter. Consider, for example, what happens to an old Western chestnut as it gets told by Huck:

> . . . I've always reckoned that looking at the new moon over your left shoulder is one of the carelessest and foolishest things a body can do. Old Hank Bunker done it once and bragged about it; and in less than two years he got drunk and fell off of a shot-tower, and spread himself out so that he was just a kind of layer, as you may say; and they slid him edgeways between two barn doors for a coffin, and buried him so, so they say, but I didn't see it. Pap told me. But anyway it all come of looking at the moon that way, like a fool.   (chap. 10)

Here the story becomes in part a revelation of Pap's character. More than that, as filtered through Huck's consciousness—his worry over new moons and his concern that the implausible details not be attributed to him—the original hilarity gets transmuted into something almost tender. Nothing of this sort has happened before, even in *Tom Sawyer*.

In like manner Huck's simplicity forces a new subtlety on Twain's satire. (I use the term *simplicity* here to indicate what is possibly more accurately suggested by the expression "the folk mind": a mind which is at once limited in knowledge and inept in abstract speculation but which is still deeply and profoundly aware of those elementary principles which give life meaning and make it tolerable.) Patently Huck does not know enough about politics, economics, and such to serve as satirist. What is more, he would make an implausible one even if properly informed since his inclination is to accept life rather than to denounce it. Substantially, therefore, the method of direct satire is closed to Twain.

But the indirect method is richly open and Twain makes the most of it. He gives to Huck those simple folk insights which in the end are the basis of his own mature reflection. Like Twain, Huck values what is useful, what is comfortable, and what is kindly. There is an obvious falsity about attaching grand labels to Huck, but it may be worth noticing that bundled up in him are the most elementary principles of utilitarianism, hedonism, and humanitarianism, and that when these principles clash the humanitarian principle prevails. Thus in Huck Twain has created a character perfectly equipped for direct or implied satire. Huck's standards are so uncomplicated and so indisputably praiseworthy that his very presence becomes a rebuke to conventional values and behavior. His practicality makes Tom's flights of fancy completely ridiculous; his hedonism makes the materialism of the Mississippi valley seem petty and futile; and his humanitarianism makes the mores and institutions of his time seem unspeakably hypocritical and cruel. To achieve his satirical intent in *Huckleberry Finn,* therefore, Twain need only show Huck acting in accord with his principles.

The most readily apparent effect on the style of this shift to indirect satire is that the narrative flow is no longer repeatedly interrupted for ridicule or denunciation. When it *is* interrupted, as when Twain stops to burlesque the artistic accomplishments of Emmeline Grangerford, there is still a general relevance. The rhetoric of direct satire which is inappropriate to Huck is either dropped, toned down, or put into the mouths of other characters, like Colonel Sherburn, where (as with the humor) it becomes primarily a revelation of character. In short, because of Huck's nature the satire, like the humor, becomes more restrained, more subtly contrived, and in the end more compelling.

Seeing the world through Huck's eyes also forces Twain into a more consistently pictorial style than he has used before. Huck is a boy, as every reader knows, of remarkable sensory perception. His concern is primarily with the facts of experience and not with generalizations drawn from the facts. And his mind, largely uncluttered with adult preconceptions, sees every experience as something fresh and new. It sees it realistically, too, for Huck is just as aware of the dangers as he is of the beauties. As Edgar M. Branch has put it, "Sensuous delight and apprehension are the twin overtones of his perception." [10] Such a viewpoint forces upon Twain an undeviating concern with the specific and concrete. The result is a style in which—and I do not exaggerate—almost every subject has a concrete referent and in which the verbs are exploited for their connotative power even more spectacularly than before. Notice a few of these verbs: "It looked late and it *smelt* late. . . . They *swarmed* up in front of Sherburn's palings. . . . The racket stopped and the wave *sucked* back. . . . The crowd *washed* back sudden and then *broke* all apart and went tearing off every which way."

Whatever other effects Huck has on Twain's style, however, easily the most important is that he forces Twain into the vernacular. Having Huck tell the story in anything but his own dialect would be preposterous.

[10] *The Literary Apprenticeship of Mark Twain* (Urbana, Ill., 1950), p. 209.

What strikes one first about the dialect in *Huckleberry Finn*, I suppose, is its colloquial authenticity. This is, of course, no accident. Twain had an extraordinary ear for dialect and had been practicing with it in writing, if we want to be literal, ever since he sent in his first piece to Shillaber's *Carpet-Bag* in 1852. As he composed in dialect, he frequently spoke many of the lines over and over until he was quite sure that he had them right. The result in *Huckleberry Finn* is that he not only discriminates between dialects but between modifications of the same dialect. And within the speech of a single character he indicates sound differences due to stress and the position in the sentence. Just as important, he catches the drawling rhythms of his characters with uncanny effectiveness. The sentences are the shortest that he uses anywhere. About half of them in the narrative passages begin with the subject. The great majority of the others begin with words that have primarily a coordinating effect, such as *and, but, so, then, well,* and *anyways.* Fewer than one-tenth begin with an introductory clause or phrase, and most of these are phrases indicating time or place. Very rarely do sentences in dialogue begin with an introductory clause or phrase, though a number begin with nonsense words like *why* and *well* or with imperative verbs.

What must be clear is that Twain's rhythms are dependent primarily upon parallelism—parallelism of sentences as well as of elements within the sentence. He regulates tempo by varying the length of the elements and the complexity of the parallelism itself. In so doing he not only effects a difference in tempo between dialogue and narrative but a difference within the narrative itself. George Mayberry has made a detailed analysis of Huck's description of the circus and has discovered that the sentence rhythm is adapted to the gait of the horses and the activities of the performers. The sentence elements first come in twos, then in threes; then there is a quick acceleration to a climax followed by a drop to a spondaic ending.[11]

Although the writing of *Huckleberry Finn* has an authentic colloquial ring, it is not simply the recording of actual talk. Twain himself, in writing to Edward Bok, remarked on the difference between writing and speaking: "The moment 'talk' is put into print you recognize that it is not what it was when you heard it; you perceive that an immense something has disappeared from it. That is its soul." What is left, he continues, is "a pallid, stiff, and repulsive cadaver." [12] No one would call Huck's talk cadaverous. It is casual, to be sure, but its casualness is so heightened that some are willing to call it folk poetry. This almost magical blend of the casual and the poetic, which avoids flatness on the one hand and mannered intensity on the other, is easier to illustrate than to describe. In the following passage, however, we can see at least some of the elements that make the blend possible.

> Once or twice of a night we would see a steamboat slipping along in the dark, and now and then she would belch a whole world of sparks up out of her chimbleys, and they would rain down in the river and look awful pretty; then she would turn a corner and her lights would wink out and her pow-wow shut off and leave the river still again; and by and by her waves would get to us a long time after

[11] "Reading and Writing," *New Republic*, CX (May 1, 1944), 608.
[12] *Mark Twain's Letters*, II, 504.

she was gone and joggle the raft a bit, and after that **you**
wouldn't hear nothing for you couldn't tell how long,
except maybe frogs or something.   (chap. 19)

Pushing the style toward the poetic are elements like these:
the richly suggestive imagery, the connotative verbs, the economy
of statement, the combination of introductory adverbial expressions and carefully molded parallelisms which create a
slow, sustained, and quiet rhythm; and the over-all unity of
effect which is so appropriate to the material. Holding the
style to the casual are elements like these: the semi-local idioms,
the phonetic spelling and the mistake in grammar, the shift
from "we" to "you"; and, especially, such imprecise expressions
as "whole world of sparks," "awful pretty," and "except maybe
frogs or something."

In forcing Twain to find dialect locutions Huck causes him to
abandon his bookish expressions. The "pretty" wording of the
conventional nature description, beginning to die out in *Tom
Sawyer,* now disappears altogether. Twain now observes through
Huck and reports what he sees in Huck's words, not in the
words of a chromo lover. Happily one misses, too, the hackneyed
phrasing that has to some degree blunted the style of all
Twain's books up to this one. Huck's dialect simply will not
accommodate the old clichés. And the "soft" wording of the
sentimental scenes almost disappears. In *Tom Sawyer,* Tom,
peeking in on grieving Aunt Polly, hears her pray for him
"touchingly" and "appealingly." He "lingers" over her while she
is asleep and finally bends and kisses her "faded lips." When
Huck says good-bye to Mary Jane Wilks, however, about all

that happens is that his eyes "water a little." Even when she promises to pray for him, he reacts admiringly but nonsentimentally:

> Pray for me! I reckoned if she knowed me she'd take a job that was more nearer her size. But I bet she done it, just the same—she was that kind. She had the grit to pray for Judas if she took the notion—there warn't no backdown to her, I judge. You may say what you want to, but in my opinion she had more sand in her than any girl I ever see; in my opinion she was just full of sand. (chap. 28)

There is no need in this paper to get tangled in the controversy over whether the last ten chapters contribute to the value of the book or lessen it. There is the possibility, however, that one point about these chapters might be relevant here. *Huckleberry Finn* is a modified frame story, with Tom the major character in the first three chapters and the last ten and Huck the major character in the large central portion. Technically the point of view does not change since Huck tells the entire story. But in effect it exerts less control over Twain in the frame elements where Tom, as the focal point, makes it relatively easy for Twain to carry the story into parody. Likewise the style *per se* does not change, but it is not so impressive in the frame elements since it is expended there upon material of less consequence.

We hardly need go back and labor the main point again. Huck, at least in the central part of the book, provides Twain with precisely the kind of detached and limited point of view that his imagination needs, and the result is his finest stylistic achievement. Indeed, if we are to believe Ernest Hemingway it is the most influential prose style in American literature.[13]

4

At first glance Hank Morgan seems to offer a point of view for *A Connecticut Yankee* that is about as detached and sharply restricted as the one Huck gives to *Huckleberry Finn*. Hank is not a boy, to be sure, but on the other hand he is not a man of broad education and sophistication. When he first wakes up in Camelot he is in his thirties; he has been a blacksmith, a horse-doctor, a mechanic, and finally a superintendent in a Connecticut arms factory; he has apparently read little and traveled not at all. By his own admission he is so practical that he is "nearly barren of sentiment." Twain's initial intention, then, is to view the arch-romance of "sixth-century" England through the eyes of a character as unromantic as one can imagine. But he does not write four chapters before he bursts through his persona and takes over the story himself. Hank Morgan remains as the narrator, but the point of view, the basic attitudes, and the language are Twain's.

This happens partly because Twain does not understand or even respect his narrator. All the elements that gave Huck reality and individuality are lacking here: a knowledge of the lore of his own religion; the local idioms, allusions, and slang; the regional pronunciation. Huck knows the jargon of the river and uses it; Hank Morgan, despite his background, employs

[13] See his much-quoted passage in the first chapter of *The Green Hills of Africa:* "All modern American literature comes from one book by Mark Twain called *Huckleberry Finn.*"

almost no shop talk. As a matter of fact, Hank's humor and general orientation are more Western than Eastern.

Twain seems to be able to conceive of the Yankee only as a stereotype, not as a flesh and blood Connecticut mechanic. What is more, it is a stereotype that he does not especially admire. In the book itself he attacks the excessively practical and moralistic person, and to Dan Beard, his illustrator, he confided that his Yankee was an "ignoramus."

Even if Twain had understood and respected his narrator, however, it is still doubtful that he would have maintained the identity, for his purposes in writing the book were too diverse and confused. At first the story was to be only a genial, tall-tale farce based on the Arthurian legend; then it was to be a satire on English traditions and institutions; finally it was both of these plus a commentary on America and mankind in general. It seems doubtful that any narrowly focused or detached point of view could have been accommodated to all that Twain wanted to jam into the book with a pen, as he said, "warmed up in hell." In any event, the result was almost inevitable: despite the Yankee narrator *A Connecticut Yankee* turns out to be closer in both point of view and style to *Innocents Abroad* than to *Huckleberry Finn*.

Like *Innocents Abroad,* such uniformity as the style of the *Connecticut Yankee* possesses it gains from its basic colloquialism, but it is a badly battered colloquialism before the book comes to an end. According to the role that Twain forces the Yankee to play, the narration displays the exaggerations, raciness, and wild climaxes of the western raconteur; the over-obvious contrivances of the burlesquer; the silly solemnities of the buffoon; the terse aphorisms of the crackerbarrel philosopher; the soggy emotion of the sentimentalist; and the sarcasm, broad irony, and vituperation of the satirist.

To take one of these roles, consider those passages in which the Yankee serves as raconteur. In these his style is at its liveliest. The incidents are molded for climax, and the words—especially the verbs—are dynamic. For sheer movement, vigor, color, and climax, some of the dramatic incidents in the book represent the finest in the western tall story tradition. And this despite the fact that even these passages are weakened by the clichés that plague the book as a whole. The climax of the restoration of the fountain in the Valley of Holiness is typical:

> Then I touched off the hogshead of rockets, and a vast fountain of dazzling lances of fire vomited itself toward the zenith with a hissing rush, and burst in mid-sky into a storm of flashing jewels! One mighty groan of terror started up from the massed people—then suddenly broke into a wild hosannah of joy—for there, fair and plain in the uncanny glare, they saw the freed water leaping forth! The old abbot could not speak a word, for tears and the chokings in his throat; without utterance of any sort, he folded me in his arms and mashed me. It was more eloquent than speech. And harder to get over, too, in a country where there were really no doctors that were worth a damaged nickel.   (chap. 23)

Twain seldom allows the Yankee to serve as raconteur very long. Invariably he turns him into a satirist and the narration into anything from gentle spoofing to angry denunciation. The satire takes many forms: aphorisms, incidents, essays, sermons, and bits and pieces of vituperation. But whatever the form, the style is almost always characterized by emotional excess. When Twain attacks a character he beats him (or her) to a literary pulp. Morgan le Fay, for example is Satan, Vesuvius, and an ass; she is "loaded to the eye-balls with cold malice"; she is "hypercritical, murderous, rapacious, and morally rotten." Similarily, when he becomes sympathetic with a character the style grows maudlin. One young woman condemned unfairly to be hanged is "friendless" and her case "piteous." As the noose is adjusted around her neck she "devours" the baby in her arms, "wildly kissing it and snatching it to her face and her breast and drenching it with her tears, and half moaning, half shrieking all the while." She implores one more kiss: "it is the dying that begs it." She gets it and almost "smothers" the child. At the last minute a priest promises to look out for it.

> You should have seen her face then! Gratitude? Lord, what do you want with words to express that? Words are only painted fire; a look is the fire itself. She gave the look, and carried it away to the treasury of heaven, where all things that are divine belong. (chap. 15)

What is probably more disconcerting about the satire than its emotional excesses is that it almost always dissolves into buffoonery. The narrator is forced to lay aside his lance and put on the cap and bells. The attack on medieval cruelty in the Morgan le Fay chapters is blunted because Hank Morgan himself suggests the hanging of the orchestra that played *In the Sweet Bye and Bye*. ("A little concession, now and then, where it can do no harm is the wise policy.") The pathetic toothless prisoners released from the dungeon are pursued by Sir Madok

selling Peterson's Prophylactic Toothbrushes. And any indignation which develops over the wanton hanging of the slaves
(and almost of the king and the boss) is dissipated by the
arrival of Sir Launcelot and his followers on bicycles. The
style in such passages shifts as abruptly as the role of the
narrator. One moment we are treated to an obviously contrived
attempt to produce concentrated horror:

> There was a jerk, and the slave hung dangling; dangling
> and hideously squirming, for his limbs were not tied.

Within a few lines, however, Hank is sounding exactly like
Tom Sawyer:

> "On your knees, every rascal of you, and salute the king!
> Who fails shall sup in hell tonight!"

I always use that high style when I'm climaxing an effect.
Sometimes the buffoon and the satirist blend together with
astonishing results. At one point in the story, in three consecutive
paragraphs the Yankee narrator sounds like a Malory ("he
lightly took his spear and gat him hence"), a sentimental
novelist ("They could remember him as he was in the freshness
and strength of his young manhood, when he kissed his child
and delivered it to its mother's hands and went away into that
long oblivion"), an American rustic ("when you can say that
of a man, he has struck bottom, I reckon"), and an essayist
gifted with erratic literary elegance (". . . all gentle cant and
philosophizing to the contrary notwithstanding, no people in
the world ever did achieve their freedom by goody-goody talk
and moral suasion").

Taken as a whole, the writing in *A Connecticut Yankee*,
despite its basic colloquialism, is just about as patchwork a

production as the ill-defined point of view should lead us to expect. Its appeal is in its profusion, in the variety and extremes of its effects. It is not dull but it is tiring. And as the book proceeds it grows progressively less interesting and effective. Like the other books discussed here, therefore, *A Connecticut Yankee* indicates that Twain's style is extraordinarily responsive to his point of view. More specifically—and here I return to my central proposition—it leads one almost inevitably to conclude that Twain's style flourishes only to the extent that his point of view is both detached and sharply restricted.

Charles R. Crow

The Style of Henry James:

The Wings of the Dove

The style of Henry James: how do we face the whole of this exacting subject? We do not, usually. To do it is to confront the writings of fifty years, some forty volumes of fiction alone. Luckily James has justified a narrowing of focus. He has given us "styles": an early, a middle (perhaps), and a late (certainly). Keep to the early or the middle, prudence would say—to go beyond is to enter legendary trouble. Yet that is where this paper will go, though not all the way.

I shall stay with one James novel from the late period, *The Wings of the Dove,* published in 1902. *The Ambassadors* and *The Golden Bowl* are equally inviting, but for other occasions. My purpose with *The Wings of the Dove* is to inspect its style at work, and my specific aim is to question how flexible the prose is, how flexible for expressing differences in movement and tone through the 764 pages. This means looking at passages that are long enough to reveal movement and tone but that are, unfortunately, excerpts. And it means neglecting dialogue altogether. My procedure is without question too simple for the bigness of *The Wings of the Dove*. The excerpts give only scattered notions of the range of effects in the novel. Yet they may serve to test the rightness of an old and enduring impression: that the later style of Henry James is all one thing, everywhere a slow, elaborate monotone. Once, we know, that was a joke. Now it is not. We see well enough that the James prose is, after all, the means by which come those insights we now value in James. We are likely to take the insights and say little about the prose. We do look at James's images, and we look at his revisions of early novels with touches of a late manner. But we may still be embarrassed about the prose in the later novels. We encourage embarrassment, perhaps, by our feeling that James's way with words and sentences outside the novels—in the prefaces, the later letters to friends, the later notebooks—is one with his way in the later novels. In a broad sense it would have to be, of course. I ask, though, whether the art of the novel does not exact from James more pressure to vary this later manner than we have commonly acknowledged.

To start an answer, I turn to the passages in *The Wings of the Dove* that introduce, in different chapters, the three principal characters. Here is Kate Croy waiting in her father's lodgings for her father to appear:

> She stared into the tarnished glass too hard indeed to be staring at her beauty alone. She readjusted the poise of her black, closely-feathered hat; retouched, beneath it, the thick fall of her dusky hair; kept her eyes, aslant, no less on her beautiful averted than on her beautiful presented oval. She was dressed altogether in black, which gave an even tone, by contrast, to her clear face and made her hair more harmoniously dark. Outside, on the balcony, her eyes

showed as blue; within, at the mirror, they showed almost as black. She was handsome, but the degree of it was not sustained by items and aids; a circumstance moreover playing its part at almost any time in the impression she produced. The impression was one that remained, but as regards the sources of it no sum in addition would have made up the total. She had stature without height, grace without motion, presence without mass. Slender and simple, frequently soundless, she was somehow always in the line of the eye—she counted singularly for its pleasure. More "dressed," often, with fewer accessories, than other women, or less dressed, should occasion require, with more, she probably could not have given the key to these felicities. They were mysteries of which her friends were conscious— those friends whose general explanation was to say that she was clever, whether or no it were taken by the world as the cause or as the effect of her charm. If she saw more things than her fine face in the dull glass of her father's lodgings, she might have seen that, after all, she was not herself a fact in the collapse. She didn't judge herself cheap, she didn't make for misery. Personally, at least, she was not chalk-marked for the auction. She hadn't given up yet, and the broken sentence, if she was the last word, *would* end with a sort of meaning.[1]   (I, 5-6)

Much, here, invites close comment: the point of view, certainly, and the tone that is an appeal for intent, sympathetic scrutiny of Kate. But the movement of the sentences concerns

---

[1] All quotations from *The Wings of the Dove* are from the edition of Charles Scribner's Sons (New York, 1945). Italics are James's.

us now. It is a forward stride with few interruptions to straight progress and those only for a second: "by contrast," "should occasion require," "after all." As we look at the sentences separately we notice things done to speed them. That first one, packed as it is with adjectives, might have been cumbersome. But the adjectives take momentum through differences of stress, of distribution. "She readjusted the poise of her black, closely-feathered hat; retouched, beneath it, the thick fall of her dusky hair. . . ." There is the simple modification by adjectives ahead of their noun, at first in a slow coalescing ("black, closely-feathered hat") and then in a quickening ("thick fall of her dusky hair") as the nouns come sooner. The sentence goes on: ". . . kept her eyes, aslant, no less on her beautiful averted than on her beautiful presented oval." The adjectives are now in suspended modification, with strong taps of stress in repetition and balance ("averted . . . presented"; "beautiful . . . beautiful"). And these differences of adjective stress are pulled into the straight progress of the sentence by the main syntax of compounded verbs: "She readjusted . . . retouched . . . kept." In sentences that follow, briskness with adjectives takes other ways. There is the sharp ending with an adjective in "Outside, on the balcony, her eyes showed as blue; within, at the mirror, they showed almost as black." And there is the pliant use of adjectives to start off: "Slender and simple, frequently soundless, she was somehow always in the line of the eye. . . ." There is the sentence between these that has no adjectives at all: "She had stature without height, grace without motion, presence without mass." The abruptness of this sentence may remind us that in the whole passage no sentence seems especially long, and that much of the force comes in short clauses: "She didn't judge herself cheap, she didn't make for misery." This is the Henry James whose later style is projecting the hard vitality of Kate with no fuss.

Something of what we think of as Jamesian fuss may come from my next excerpt. Here is the introduction of Merton Densher:

He was a longish, leanish, fairish young Englishman, not unamenable, on certain sides, to classification—as for instance by being a gentleman, by being rather specifically one of the educated, one of the generally sound and generally pleasant; yet, though to that degree neither extraordinary nor abnormal, he would have failed to play straight into an observer's hands. He was young for the House of Commons, he was loose for the army. He was refined, as might have been said, for the city, and, quite apart from the cut of his cloth, he was sceptical, it might have been felt, for the church. . . . The difficulty with Densher was that he looked vague without looking weak—idle without looking empty. It was the accident, possibly, of his long legs, which were apt to stretch themselves; of his straight hair and his well-shaped head, never, the latter, neatly smooth, and apt, into the bargain, at the time of quite other calls upon it, to throw itself suddenly back and, supported behind by his uplifted arms and interlocked hands, place him for unconscionable periods in communion with the ceiling, the tree-tops, the sky. He was in short visibly absent-minded, irregularly clever, liable to drop what was near and to take up what was far; he was more a respecter, in general, than a follower of custom. He suggested above all, however, that wondrous state of youth in which the elements, the metals more or less precious, are so in fusion and fermentation that the question of the final stamp, the pressure that fixes the value, must wait for comparative coolness. . . .   (I, 54-55)

The view is the narrator's, though it is becoming Densher's, too, since the chapter has already started through his awareness. In what I have quoted, the tone strikes immediately: a tone of amiable indulgence for contradictions in Densher. It is almost jocosely airy in "longish, leanish, fairish," as if coming in club-room talk among men and as if here, in the novel, catching a man's view first of this Densher who is to be so surrounded by petticoats. The airiness is sustained in the series of rejected speculations (some of which I have not quoted) about what Densher's profession could be. And the statements about his head are turned towards the inconsequential by the word "unconscionable" in "place him for unconscionable periods in communion with the ceiling, the tree-tops, the sky." Yet "communion" and the range of suggestion (if the tone would allow) in "ceiling," "tree-tops," "sky," give a hint of what will later emerge as serious meanings. They are not emerging now. As the tone and, indeed, the summarizing statement say, here is a person awaiting "the final stamp, the pressure that fixes the value."

The sentences that convey this impression are lesisurely, perhaps devious, with something of the hedging so often thought of as James's later manner. The first sentence may be in fact a kind in James to start impatience if one stands aside from it.

Densher is "not unamenable, on certain sides, to classification. . . ." Why the roundabout "not unamenable," and why, even after that, the delay in getting to "classification"? Why not simply "in some ways not hard to classify"? And Densher, still in this sentence, is "one of the generally sound and generally pleasant." Why make so much of "generally" and give such resonance otherwise to what is only a classification? Impatience is allayed, true, by the rush of unresonant words at the end of the sentence: "he would have failed to play straight into an observer's hands." Exactly. Why not say so right off? But we take what we get in James, and what we get may not let us stand aside after all for impatience. In the context the sentence offers signals for the kind of attention to be given Densher. After "longish, leanish, fairish young Englishman," jauntily positive with no mystery about it, the sentence begins to say "Wait! Look again and be baffled with the rest of us." "Not unamenable, on certain sides, to classification" puts a "Well, yes" and a "Well, no" together in a way of meaning both at once, as our impatient revision, "in some ways not hard to classify," does not. And "one of the generally sound and generally pleasant" yields interesting precision: "generally" takes implications of "usually so, but not always" and also implications of "genus"—the English gentleman—since there is talk of classification. All this may be worth some resonance. We come back to the tone, the air of affable invitation to look closely at this young man though to smile, as yet, at how hard he is to pin down. This is the tone and such are the sentences that turn Densher around and around before us until what is "not unamenable" will take darker meanings in Kate's use of it.

To turn to the passage in the novel that first shows us Milly Theale is to find ourselves in a new region of effect. For one matter, we are now deep in the novel, and the narrator has given over, at this point, to Mrs. Stringham's view of things. Mrs. Stringham's memories bring Milly forward for us, Milly as Mrs. Stringham the New Englander first saw her in Boston.

> Mrs. Stringham was never to forget—for the moment had not faded, nor the infinitely fine vibration it set up in any degree ceased—her own first sight of the striking apparition, then unheralded and unexplained: the slim, constantly pale, delicately haggard, anomalously, agreeably angular young person, of not more than two-and-twenty in spite of her marks, whose hair was somehow exceptionally red even for the real thing, which it innocently confessed to being, and whose clothes were remarkably black even for robes of mourning, which was the meaning they expressed. It was New York mourning, it was New York hair, it was a New York history, confused as yet, but multitudinous, of the loss of parents, brothers, sisters, almost every human appendage, all on a scale and with a sweep that had required the greater stage; it was a New York legend of affecting, of romantic isolation, and, beyond everything, it was by most accounts, in respect to the mass of money so piled on the girl's back, a set of New York possibilities. She was alone, she was stricken, she was rich, and, in particular, she was strange—a combination in itself of a nature to engage Mrs. Stringham's attention. . . .   (I, 117–18)

An effect of this passage is named at its start: Milly is an "apparition," and the moment of seeing her is, for Mrs. Stringham, still present as an "infinitely fine vibration." The passage projects, in fact, just that—a *vibration* of darkly appealing strangeness. There is a vibrating, an oscillating, between what seeks to localize ("angular," "red hair," "New York") and what escapes localizing entirely ("apparition," "delicately haggard," "legend," "alone," "stricken"). The vibration is almost stopped by Mrs. Stringham's asperity: "in respect to the mass of money piled on the girl's back, a set of New York possibilities." But the next sentence starts it again with "alone," "stricken," "rich," and "strange." The suggestions of Shakespeare's *The Tempest* are inescapable here, as F. O. Matthiessen has pointed out concerning another passage where "rich" and "strange" recur together.[2] The paragraph I am quoting ends, beyond my quotation, with ironies about Mrs. Stringham's pride of exclusive insight unavailable in Boston; but the ironies do not stop the vibrancy of the impression of Milly.

James's style, then, manages vibration. But that is not the whole of it. The sentences give this passage actually a groundwork of downrightness. The first one does start lingeringly: "Mrs. Stringham was never to forget—for the moment had not faded, nor the infinitely fine vibration it set up in any degree ceased. . . ." Yet even here the "in any degree ceased" brings a steady sense of measuring, slight but definite. The measuring, the estimating, is rhetorically emphatic in the next sentence with its iterations: "It was New York mourning, it was New York hair, it was a New York history. . . ." This kind of emphasis is compressed in the third sentence into the bare contact clauses, "She was alone, she was stricken, she was

[2] *Henry James: The Major Phase* (New York, 1944), p. 60.

rich, and, in particular, she was strange. . . ." Then, in the same sentence, the effect is dryly loosened by "a combination in itself of a nature to engage Mrs. Stringham's attention." The loosening is James's modulation into the ironies about New England that follow. What the passage has offered is a counterpointing: vibrations in the view of Milly are played against a steadiness in the mind that is viewing, the mind that frames these sentences —Mrs. Stringham's, in the illusion of the novel.

Parts of three paragraphs in James's later style have now been before us. There is no denying that their style is elaborate. But is it a monotone? Not one tone but three have been dramatized, and each has involved a different movement of sentences. The reader may protest that these passages are not typical, that the novel does not often break into such displays. What of the rest—the pages, for sharpest test, that carry dramatic action forward? Do they carry it, or are they all one Jamesian rumble? "Dramatic action" is a treacherous phrase to be turned upon James. As we know, everything, everywhere in a later James novel is likely to be an action with its own quality of drama. We shall not find in *The Wings of the Dove* much that is narration of entirely overt action; the action of someone's mind will always be there too. But, for our interest in flexibility of prose, let us look at two passages of crisis that involve outer and inner action. The first occurs just after Densher proposes, in Venice, that Kate come to him in his rooms if he is to go through with the plan of marrying Milly for her money. The place is the Piazza San Marco, where Densher and Kate seize a chance to talk while Mrs. Lowder and Mrs. Stringham shop in the gallery. In the episode are overtones of Densher's passion for Kate, of his horror at the plans concerning Milly, and of his revolt from the furtiveness of the whole business.

> On possessing himself of her arm he had made her turn, so that they faced afresh to St. Mark's, over the great presence of which his eyes moved while she twiddled her parasol. She now, however, made a motion that confronted them finally with the opposite end. Then only she spoke—"Please take your hand out of my arm." He understood at once: she had made out in the shade of the gallery the issue of the others from their place of purchase. So they went to them side by side, and it was all right. The others had seen them as well and waited for them, complacent enough, under one of the arches. They themselves too—he argued that Kate would argue—looked perfectly ready, decently patient, properly accommodating. They suggested nothing worse—always by Kate's system—than a pair of the children of a supercivilised age making the best of an awkwardness. . . .
>
> (II, 220)

The first sentence quoted is worth a close look at what James does in its action. The beginning of the sentence turns the two to face the church. What follows, then, holds the action of his eyes and her parasol to a syntax of modifying "St. Mark's": "so that they faced afresh to St. Mark's, over the great presence of which his eyes moved while she twiddled her parasol." By its structure the sentence suspends the church, a "great presence," above Densher's awareness of its presence and Kate's action of trivial disregard. Something of the dramatic contrast, that is, in the attitudes of these two is caught and fixed for a moment in the structure of the sentence. The next sentences put Densher and Kate into motion. In the turn from St. Mark's, in the curtness of Kate's request, and in "So they went to them side by side . . ." there is Densher's sense of movement in unwilling tension. Then the released breath, "and it was all right." The sentences return, as do Densher's mental powers, to elaborateness—when, dramatically, *it* is all right.

We glance now at a brief part of a passage that gives us Milly in emotional collapse. She is talking with Lord Mark in her Venetian palace; it is his question that brings her to crisis.

"Do you mean," Lord Mark presently asked, "that you're really not well?"

They were at the window, pausing, lingering, with the fine old faded palaces opposite and the slow Adriatic tide beneath; but after a minute, and before she answered, she had closed her eyes to what she saw and, unresistingly, dropped her face into her arms, which rested on the coping. She had fallen to her knees on the cushion of the window-place, and she leaned there, in a long silence, with her forehead down. She knew that her silence was itself too straight an answer, but it was beyond her now to say that she saw her way. . . .   (II, 163–64)

These sentences need no analysis. By their gatherings and their pauses they make their comment on what James's style can do. Style, here, does carry dramatic meaning.

All these excerpts, a reader may still say, evade giving a fair view of what the style on most pages of *The Wings of the Dove* is. There are those stretches and stretches of prose that, perversely. James calls the "picture" parts of the novel, the prose that draws out the thoughts, the reflections of one of the characters.

Is there not in these the staple prose of the novel, and is it not monotonous? The question concerns arrangement, perhaps, proportions of emphasis, more than it concerns prose style. The style in these passages does direct attention variously. To demonstrate this impression is difficult, granted the lengths of the passages that must be considered. Any attentive reader of James will recognize, though, how typical the following sentences are, taken from a long interior monologue: typical not in movement, for that varies everywhere, but in the aids to the reader that James so carefully puts into them. Here are Densher's thoughts while he is talking with Milly in London. James does not give the conversation at this point—just the drift of it as it comes through Densher's thoughts.

The question the girl had quickly disposed of—"Oh, it was nothing: I'm all right, thank you!"—was one he was glad enough to be able to banish. It was not at all, in spite of the appeal Kate had made to him on it, his affair; for his interest had been invoked in the name of compassion, and the name of compassion was exactly what he felt himself at the end of two minutes forbidden so much as to whisper. He had been sent to see her in order to be sorry for her, and how sorry he might be, quite privately, he was yet to make out. Didn't that signify, however, almost not at all?—inasmuch as, whatever his upshot, he was never to let her know it. Thus the ground was unexpectedly cleared; though it was not till a slightly longer time had passed that he made sure, at first with amusement and then with a sort of respect, of what had most operated. Extraordinarily, quite amazingly, he began to see that if his pity hadn't had to yield to still other things it would have had to yield quite definitely to her own. That was the way the case had turned round: he had made his visit to be sorry for her, but he would repeat it—if he did repeat it—in order that she might be sorry for *him*. . . .   (II, 82)

What keeps this going is the unmistakable impression that a mind is moving ahead, a mind playing discursively with the situation and keeping its own processes in view. In the style, rhetorical means for conveying momentum abound. There are the guiding elements: "he was yet to make out"; "Thus the ground was unexpectedly cleared"; "That was the way the case had turned round." There are the repetitions of key phrases ("the name of compassion"), and there are the reversals of meaning worked out with crisp openness and even with italics ("to be sorry for her . . . that she might be sorry for *him*.") Plainly James wants this prose to be out in the open, for all that it goes on in Densher's mind. But it does go on for eight pages in this passage. Whether, for all James's care, it can keep a steady hold on the reader depends, no doubt, on James's care with other matters—the varieties and accumulations of meaning that the prose conveys. The prose itself is flexible.

My last excerpt is offered to counter any impression I may have given that James's style in this book is merely facile. The style has its obstacles, its strains, its tuggings for control beneath the surface. The passage I shall quote comes towards the end of the novel. Milly has died in Venice on Christmas eve. Densher on the same day is in London, waiting for word of her death. He has received on this day a letter from Milly, a letter which he has not opened. In his mind, what Milly stands for confronts what Kate stands for and what he has done, through Kate, to injure Milly. He is in a Christmas eve vigil of the spirit, and his spirit is in paralysis between alternatives. He makes no decision, yet when Christmas day dawns he feels himself "somehow determined." Gradually, through fifty more pages, we perceive with Densher what has happened: in the Christmas dawn, redemption—in meanings of Milly—has come to his spirit. The Christmas eve vigil is presented in a single paragraph. Its sentences approach, as they seldom do in James, the compression of a poem. Here is a part of the paragraph:

> It was his difficulty for the moment that he was face to face with alternatives, and that it was scarce even a question of turning from one to the other. They were not in a perspective in which they might be compared and considered; they were, by a strange effect, as close as a pair of monsters of whom he might have felt on either cheek the hot breath and the huge eyes. He saw them at once and but by looking straight before him; he wouldn't, for that matter, in his cold apprehension, have turned his head by an inch. So it was that his agitation was still—was not, for the slow hours, a matter of restless motion. He lay long, after the event, on the sofa on which, extinguishing at a touch the white light of convenience that he hated, he had thrown himself without undressing. He stared at the buried day and wore out the time; with the arrival of the Christmas dawn, moreover, late and grey, he felt himself somehow determined. . . .   (II, 381–82)

It is not easy to describe the style of this passage. If we brush aside some things, we find a tone of deeply intense engagement.

In the image of the monsters, for instance, that sentence which ends with "the hot breath and the huge eyes" compels rhythmic pressure: there is hovering stress over each pair of monosyllables, the stress accentuated by the light "and the" between the pairs. This pressure works, of course, to urge gravity of meanings—meanings, in Densher's alternatives, of passion and conscience. Pressure in another way, juxtaposition of words in paradox, comes in the sentence that begins "So it was that his agitation was still . . ."—comes with more strain than T. S. Eliot was to give it long afterwards in "At the still point of the turning world." Doubtless this whole passage of James was lodged somewhere in Mr. Eliot's mind. The section of *Burnt Norton* from which I have just quoted starts "Time and the bell have buried the day. . . ." [3] And here, in the James paragraph, is "He stared at the buried day and wore out the time. . . ." The James sentence—or at least the part of it here quoted—brings Densher's paralysis to starkest wording. Again the gravity is intensified by rhythm: "He stared at the buried day and wore out the time" would be a hexameter in stress-verse, the stresses emphasizing compression and holding it in. What the words hold are possible immensities of implication in the Christmas context. *Possible* immensities—though whether they are there I am not sure. An objective correlative may be at work. There may be something of St. Paul's "Therefore we are buried with him by baptism into death . . ." [4] or even his "That ye put off concerning the former conversation the old man, which is corrupt according to the deceitful lusts; And

[3] *Four Quartets* (New York, 1943), p. 7. James's "buried day" may be a recollection of Meredith's "Their hearts held cravings for the buried day" (*Modern Love,* L). I am indebted to Phyllis Bartlett for this suggestion.

[4] Romans 6.4.

be renewed in the spirit of your mind; and that ye put on the new man. . . ."[5] In the Quentin Anderson interpretation of this novel Densher is the "redeemed" in full religious meaning; he does "put on the new man."[6] By whatever interpretation, the Christmas eve paragraph finds Densher between something old and something new, staring at the "buried day."

But the style of the James paragraph is not Biblical, not liturgical. If there is in James what I have spoken of as gravity brought partly by tightening rhythm and by compression, there is also, mixed in, a dryness that works to keep solemnity away. The effect is not pronounced, but it is there. After the "hot breath and the huge eyes" of the monsters we read this: "He saw them at once and but by looking straight before him; he wouldn't, for that matter, in his cold apprehension, have turned his head by an inch." "For that matter"—the discursive James (or the discursive Densher) will not give up even here. After the words "So it was that his agitation was still" we read, ". . . was not, for the slow hours, a matter of restless motion." Again the "matter" —and the discursiveness—where the grave tone could have been sustained by wording it "not, for the slow hours, restless motion." But this would bring more compression than evidently James wants in an already strikingly compressed sentence. His "a matter of" loosens the sentence and dries the tone: this stillness of agitation was something beyond mere matters of restless motion. And the sentence about the buried day has the same loosening, the same change towards dryness. It continues, ". . . with the arrival of the Christmas dawn, moreover, late and grey, he

---

[5] Ephesians 4.22–24.
[6] *The American Henry James* (New Brunswick, 1957), pp. 275–80.

felt himself somehow determined." The "moreover" works the change, though "late and grey" bring back the graveness of "Christmas dawn" for a moment. What James will not do, one sees, is let intensity be entire. His style is a prose style. If the compressions, the strainings of poetry do enter, they are brought to conform.

This observation leads, if one likes, into critical views of James's later style that see it at no such workaday level as I have kept it to. Style is of course a more subtle and a more exalting achievement in James than what my concern with its flexibility has brought out. Our critics will continue to exercise their acuteness on its more embracing aspects. Yet they might stoop now and then to the concerns of this paper, watch the James style at work as craft in *The Ambassadors* and *The Golden Bowl*. They would thus remind us that James did strive to be readable. *The Wings of the Dove* is not an indulgence of private vision. It releases the motions and the tones of its meanings to the reader.

Harold C. Martin and
Richard M. Ohmann

A Selective Bibliography

The selectivity of this bibliography is in some measure qualitative. In the main, however, selection has been determined by the four following considerations. First, we decided to limit ourselves to studies written in English or about English and American literature. The rare exceptions are standard works in the field, such as Leo Spitzer's *Stilstudien*. Our decision in this matter rests not so much on the sponsorship of this volume by the *English* Institute as on the existence of excellent bibliographies for those European literatures in which most readers of this volume are likely to have a scholarly interest. The most extensive of these bibliographies is Helmut A. Hatzfeld's admirable volume, *A Critical Bibliography of the New Stylistics Applied to the Romance Literatures, 1900–1952* (Chapel Hill, N.C., 1953). For stylistic studies of German literature, pages 66–69 of Josef Körner's *Bibliographisches Handbuch des deutschen Schrifttums* (Berne, 1949) are useful. The bibliography compiled by Charles Bally, Elise Richter, Amado Alonso, and Raimundo Lida in *El impressionismo en el lenguage* (Buenos Aires, 1936) has been superseded but should be mentioned not only for its merit but also because it may be available in some libraries which lack the more comprehensive work by Hatzfeld. Mention should be made also of the journal *Trivium: Schweizerische Vierteljahrschrift für Literaturwissenschaft und Stilistik* (Zurich, 1942–53), which is a repository of articles on style.

The three other considerations can be briefly stated. We have included very few items published before 1928 and none before 1920. Most of the work done in stylistics before that date has either become classic in the field or has lost value because of methodological obsolescence. We have also restricted ourselves entirely to studies of *prose* style and have paid most attention to studies of prose style in fiction. Finally, we have excluded most quantitative analyses of imagery on the ground that, though the *way* imagery is used is certainly a matter of style, the relative frequency of water to machine images is, at best, rudimentary or peripheral.

We have included a very few grammatical and linguistic works of importance to the subject and might well have extended the list of such books to many times its length, considering their importance to anyone who intends to explore the field of stylistic analysis, but were restrained by the usual limitations of space.

Allen, Don Cameron, "Style and Certitude," *English Literary History,* XV (1948), 167–75.

Allott, Kenneth, and Miriam Allott, eds., "Introduction," *Victorian Prose 1830–1880.* London, 1956. The Pelican Book of English Prose, Vol. V.

Alonzo, Amado, "The Stylistic Interpretation of Literary Texts," *Modern Language Notes,* LVII (1942), 489–96.

Aronstein, Ph., "On Style and Styles in Languages," *American Speech,* IX (1934), 243–51.

Auerbach, Erich. Mimesis: The Representation of Reality in Western Literature, trans. by Willard Trask. Princeton, N.J., 1953.

Aurner, Robert Roy, "The History of Certain Aspects of the Structure of the English Sentence," *Philological Quarterly,* II (1923), 187–208.

Barish, Jonas A., "The Prose Style of John Lyly," *English Literary History,* XXIII (1956), 14–35.

Baum, Paull F. The Other Harmony of Prose: An Essay in English Prose Rhythm. Durham, N.C., 1952.

Beach, Joseph Warren. The Outlook for American Prose. Chicago, 1926.

Beck, Warren, "William Faulkner's Style," in *William Faulkner: Two Decades of Criticism,* ed. by Frederick J. Hoffman and Olga W. Vickery. East Lansing, Mich., 1951.

Bergler, Edmund, "Myth, Merit, and Mirage of Literary Style," *Imago,* VII (1950), 279–87.

Bevis, Dorothy, *"The Waves:* A Fusion of Symbol, Style and Thought in Virginia Woolf," *Twentieth-Century Literature,* II (1956), 5–20.

Blackmur, Richard P. Language as Gesture. New York, 1952.

Boulton, Marjorie. The Anatomy of Prose. New York, 1957.

Bowling, Lawrence Edward, "What Is the Stream of Consciousness Technique?," *PMLA,* LXV (1950), 333–45.

Bradbrook, Frank W., "Style and Judgment in Jane Austen's Novels," *Cambridge Journal,* IV (1951), 515–37.

Brower, Reuben Arthur. The Fields of Light. New York, 1951.

Brower, Reuben, ed. On Translation. Cambridge, Mass., 1959.

Brownell, W. C. The Genius of Style. New York, 1924.

——— American Prose Masters. New York, 1925.

Burke, Kenneth. A Rhetoric of Motive. New York, 1950.

——— Permanence and Change: An Anatomy of Purpose. 2d rev. ed. Los Altos, Calif., 1954. "Style," pp. 50–58.

Burkhard, Arthur. Conrad Ferdinand Meyer: The Style and the Man. Cambridge, Mass., 1932.

Chambers, Raymond Wilson. On the Continuity of English Prose from Alfred to More and His School. London, 1932, 1954.

Chandler, Zilpha Emma. An Analysis of the Stylistic Technique of Addison, Johnson, Hazlitt, and Pater. Iowa City, Ia., 1928. University of Iowa Humanistic Studies, Vol. IV, No. 3.

Collier, S. J., "Max Jacob and the 'Poème en Prose,' " *Modern Language Review,* LI (1956), 522–35.

Cope, Jackson, "Seventeenth-Century Quaker Style," *PMLA,* LXXI (1956), 725–54.

Corin, Fernand, "Steinbeck and Hemingway—A Study in Literary

Economy," *Revue des Langues vivantes,* XXIV (1958), 60–75, 153–63.

Craddock, Sister Clare Eileen. Style Theories as Found in Stylistic Studies of Romance Scholars (1900–1950). Washington, D.C., 1952. Catholic University of America Studies in Romance Languages and Literatures, Vol. XLIII.

Crane, William G. Wit and Rhetoric in the Renaissance: The Formal Basis of Elizabethan Prose Style. New York, 1938.

Croll, Morris, " 'Attic Prose' in the Seventeenth Century," *Studies in Philology,* XVIII (1921), 79–128.

———— "Muret and the History of 'Attic Prose,'" *PMLA,* XXXIX (1924), 254–309.

———— "The Baroque Style in Prose," in *Studies in English Philology: A Miscellany in Honor of F. Klaeber,* ed. by K. Malone and M. B. Rund. Minneapolis, Minn., 1929.

Daniells, Roy, "Baroque Form in English Literature," *University of Toronto Quarterly,* XIV (1945), 393–408.

Davie, Donald A., "Berkeley's Style in *Siris,*" *Cambridge Journal,* IV (1951), 427–33.

Dobrée, Bonamy. Modern Prose Style. Oxford, 1934.

Doner, Dean, "Virginia Woolf: The Service of Style," *Modern Fiction Studies,* II (1956), 1–12.

Douglas, Wallace W., "Drug Store Gothic: The Style of Robert Penn Warren," *College English,* XV (1954), 265–72.

Dyson, A. E., "A Note on Dismissive Irony," *English,* XI (1957), 222–25.

Emden, Cecil S., "Rhythmical Features in Dr. Johnson's Prose," *Review of English Studies,* XXV (1949), 38–54.

Erlich, Victor. Russian Formalism. 's-Gravenhage, 1955.

Firkins, Oscar. William Dean Howells. Cambridge, Mass., 1924.

Frances, G. Emberson, "Mark Twain's Vocabulary: A General Survey," *University of Missouri Studies,* X (No. 3, 1935), 1–53.

Freeman, F. Barron, ed. Melville's Billy Budd. Cambridge, Mass.,

1948. "Convolutions and Quiddities: Melville's Style," pp. 97–114 of Introduction.

Frey, John, "The Historical Present in Narrative Literature, Particularly in Modern German Fiction," *Journal of English and Germanic Philology*, XLV (1946), 43–66.

Friedman, Melvin J. Stream of Consciousness: A Study in Literary Method. New Haven, Conn., 1955.

Fries, Charles Carpenter. The Structure of English. New York, 1952.

Frohock, W. M., "Camus: Image, Influence and Sensibility," *Yale French Studies*, II (1949), 91–99.

Frye, Northrop. Anatomy of Criticism. Princeton, N.J., 1957. Pages 263–68, 326–37.

Glasgow, Ellen. A Certain Measure: An Interpretation of Prose Fiction. New York, 1943.

Hartwick, Harry. The Foreground of American Fiction. New York, 1934.

Hatcher, Anna G., "Syntax and the Sentence," *Word*, XII (1956), 234–250.

Hatcher, Harlan. Creating the Modern American Novel. New York, 1935.

Hatzfeld, Helmut, "Stylistic Criticism as Artminded Philology," *Yale French Studies*, II (1949), 62–70.

Heilman, Robert B., "Poetic and Prosaic: Program Notes on Opposite Numbers," *Pacific Spectator*, V (1951), 454–63.

Higashida, Chiaki, "On the Prose Style of D. H. Lawrence," *Studies in English Literature* (Tokyo University), XIX (1939), 545–56.

Holloway, John. The Victorian Sage. London, 1953.

Hopkins, Viola, "The Ordering Style of *The Age of Innocence*," *American Literature*, XXX (1958), 345–57.

Houghton, Walter. The Art of Newman's "Apologia." New Haven, Conn., 1945.

——— "The Rhetoric of T. H. Huxley," *University of Toronto Quarterly*, XVIII (1949), 159–75.

Hulme, Thomas Ernest. Notes on Language and Style, ed. by Herbert. Read. Seattle, Wash., 1929. University of Washington Chapbooks, Vol. XXV.

Humphrey, Robert. Stream of Consciousness in the Modern Novel. Berkeley, Calif., 1954.

Jakobson, Roman, "Two Aspects of Language and Two Types of Aphasic Disturbances," in R. Jakobson and M. Halle, *Fundamentals of Language.* 's-Gravenhage, 1956. Janua Linguarum, Vol. I.

Jeffersen, D. W., ed., "Introduction," *Eighteenth-Century Prose, 1700–1780.* London, 1956. The Pelican Book of English Prose, Vol. III.

Jespersen, Otto. The Philosophy of Grammar. Oxford, 1921.

Jones, Howard Mumford, "American Prose Style: 1700–1770," *Huntington Library Bulletin,* VI (1934), 115–51.

Jones, Richard F., "Science and English Prose Style in the Third Quarter of the Seventeenth Century," *PMLA,* XLV (1930), 977–1009.

Kayser, Wolfgang. Das sprachliche Kunstwerk: Eine Einführung in die Literaturwissenschaft. Berne, 1948.

Kegel, Charles, H., "Incommunicability in Salinger's *Catcher in the Rye,*" *Western Humanities Review,* XI (1957), 188–90.

Knights, L. C., "Elizabethan Prose," *Scrutiny,* II (1934), 427–38.

Knox, George, "James's Rhetoric of 'Quotes,'" *College English,* XVII (1956), 293–97.

Lambert, Mildred, "Studies in Stylistics," *American Speech,* III (1928), 173–81, 326–33; IV (1929), 28–39, 137–44, 228–43, 395–402, 477–89.

Lannering, Jan. Studies in the Prose Style of Joseph Addison. Cambridge, Mass., 1951. Essays and Studies on English Language and Literature (Uppsala), Vol. IX.

Lee, Vernon [pseud. of Violet Paget]. The Handling of Words, and Other Studies in Literary Psychology. New York, 1923.

[Levin, Harry] "Expressive Voices: The Emergence of a National Style," *Times Literary Supplement,* September 17, 1954, pp. xii–xiv.

Levin, Harry. The Power of Blackness: Hawthorne, Poe, Melville. New York, 1958.

—— Contexts in Criticism. Cambridge, Mass., 1957, "The Prose of Ernest Hemingway."

Lucas, F. L. Style. London, 1955.

Mapes, E. K., "Implications of Some Recent Studies on Style," *Revue de Littérature Comparée*, XVIII (1938), 514–33.

Martin, Howard H., " 'Style' in the Golden Age," *Quarterly Journal of Speech*, XLIII (1957), 374–82.

Marx, Leo, "The Pilot and the Passenger: Landscape Conventions and the Style of *Huckleberry Finn*," *American Literature*, XXVIII (1956), 129–46.

McFarlane, J. W., "Plasticity in Language: Some Notes on the Prose Style of Ernst Barlach," *Modern Language Review*, XLIX (1954), 451–60.

Mégroz, R. L., "Conrad's Craftsmanship," *This Quarter*, IV (1931), 130–41.

Morgan, Bayard Quincy, "Some Functions of Time in Speech," *American Speech*, XX (1945), 28–33.

Munro, Thomas, "Style in the Arts: A Method of Stylistic Analysis," *Journal of Aesthetics and Art Criticism*, V (1946), 128–58.

Munson, Gorham. Style and Form in American Prose. Garden City, N.Y., 1929.

Murry, John Middleton. The Problem of Style. Oxford, 1922.

Myers, Henry Alonso, "Style and the Man," *South Atlantic Quarterly*, XL (1941), 259–68.

Paget, Violet, *see* Lee, Vernon.

Pound, Louise, "The Dialect of Cooper's Leatherstocking," *American Speech*, II (1927), 479–88.

Quinn, Arthur Hobson. American Fiction. New York, 1936.

Rahv, Philip, "Fiction and the Criticism of Fiction," *Kenyon Review*, XVIII (1956), 276–99.

Raleigh, John Henry, "Style and Structure in Defoe's *Roxana*," *University of Kansas City Review*, XX (1953), 128–35.

Ransom, John Crowe, "The Understanding of Fiction," *Kenyon Review*, XII (1950), 189–218.

Read, Herbert. English Prose Style. New York, 1928.

Rees, G. O., "Types of Recurring Similes in Malraux's Novels," *Modern Language Notes*, LXVII (1953), 373–77.

Richards, Ivor Armstrong. Interpretation in Teaching. New York, 1938.

—— The Philosophy of Rhetoric. New York, 1936.

Riedel, F. C., "Faulkner as Stylist," *South Atlantic Quarterly*, LVI (1957), 462–79.

Roberts, Murat H., "The Science of Idiom: A Method of Inquiry Into the Cognitive Design of Language," *PMLA*, LIX (1944), 291–306.

Roellinger, Francis X., Jr., "The Early Development of Carlyle's Style," *PMLA*, LXXII (1957), 936–51.

Saidla, L. E. A. Essay for the Study of Structure and Style. New York, 1939.

Satterwhite, Joseph N., "The Tremulous Formula: Form and Technique in *Godey's* Fiction," *American Quarterly*, VIII (1956), 99–114.

Sayce, R. A. Style in French Prose. Oxford, 1953.

—— "Literature and Language," *Essays in Criticism*, VII (1957), 119–33.

Schorer, Mark, "Fiction and the 'Analogical Matrix,'" in *Critiques and Essays in Modern Fiction*, ed. by John W. Aldridge. New York, 1952.

Shannon, Edgar F., Jr., "The Present Tense in *Jane Eyre*," *Nineteenth-Century Fiction*, X (1955), 141–45.

Short, R. W., "The Sentence Structure of Henry James," *American Literature*, XVIII (1946), 71–88.

Slatoff, Walter J., "The Edge of Order: The Pattern of Faulkner's Rhetoric," *Twentieth-Century Literature*, III (1957), 107–27.

Smith, Colin, "Aspects of Destutt de Tracy's Linguistic Analysis as Adopted by Stendhal," *Modern Language Review*, LI (1956), 512–21.

Söderlind, Johannes. Verb Syntax in John Dryden's Prose. 2 vols. Cambridge, Mass., 1951, 1958. Essays and Studies on English (Uppsala), Vols. X, XIX.

Spiller, Robert E., "Cooper's Notes on Language," *American Speech,* IV (1929), 294–300.

Spitzer, Leo. Stilstudien. 2 vols. Munich, 1928.

—— Linguistics and Literary History, Essays in Stylistics. Princeton, N.J., 1948.

—— A Method of Interpreting Literature. Northampton, Mass., 1949, "Pages from Voltaire," pp. 64–101.

Sonnenschein, E. A. What Is Rhythm? Oxford, 1925.

Staton, Walter F., "Characters of Style in Elizabethan Prose," *Journal of English and Germanic Philology,* LVII (1958), 197–207.

Stevenson, Lionel, "Meredith and the Problem of Style in the Novel," *Zeitschrift für Anglistik und Amerikanistik,* VI (1958), 181–89.

Stutterheim, C. F. P., "Modern Stylistics," *Lingua,* I (1948), 410–26; III (1952), 52–68.

Sutherland, James, "Some Aspects of Eighteenth-Century Prose," in *Essays on the Eighteenth Century: Presented to David Nichol Smith in Honour of His Seventieth Birthday.* Oxford, 1945.

Sypher, Wylie. Four Stages of Renaissance Style: Transformations in Art and Literature. Garden City, N.Y., 1955.

Thomson, J. A. K. Classical Influences on English Prose. London, 1956.

Tillyard, E. M. W., "Scott's Linguistic Vagaries," *Etudes anglaises,* XI (1958), 112–18.

Troy, William, "Virginia Woolf: The Poetic Method," *Symposium,* III (1932), 53–63.

—— "Virginia Woolf: The Poetic Style," *Symposium,* III (1932), 153–56.

Ullmann, Stephen. Style in the French Novel. Cambridge, England, 1957.

Umbach, Herbert M., "The Merit of the Metaphysical Style in Donne's Easter Sermons," *English Literary History,* XII (1945), 108–29.

Uve, Peter, ed., "Introduction," *Seventeenth-Century Prose, 1620–1700*, London, 1956. The Pelican Book of English Prose, Vol. II.

VanGhent, Dorothy. The English Novel, Form and Function. New York, 1953.

Walpole, Hugh. The Art of James Branch Cabell. New York, 1920.

Wellek, René, and Austin Warren. Theory of Literature. New York, 1949, "Style and Stylistics," pp. 177–89.

Whorf, Benjamin Lee. Language, Thought, and Reality. Cambridge, Mass., and New York, 1956.

Willey, Basil. The Seventeenth Century Background. Cambridge, England, 1934, Chapter III, "Sir Thomas Browne."

Williamson, George. The Senecan Amble: A Study in Prose Form from Bacon to Collier. Chicago, 1951.

Williams, William Carlos, "The Work of Gertrude Stein," *Pagany*, I (1930), 41–46.

Wimsatt, William K. The Prose Style of Samuel Johnson. New Haven, 1941.

—— Philosophic Words. New Haven, 1948.

—— The Verbal Icon. Lexington, Ky., 1954. "Verbal Style: Logical and Counterlogical."

Wyld, Henry Cecil. Modern Colloquial English. London, 1920, Chapters I and X.

Yule, G. Udny. The Statistical Study of Literary Vocabulary. Cambridge, England, 1944.

Zoellner, Robert H., "Faulkner's Prose Style in *Absalom, Absalom!*," *American Literature*, XXX (No. 4, 1959), 486–502.

Supervising Committee, the English Institute, 1958

The Program

September 2 through September 5, 1958
Conferences

I. THE LAST VICTORIANS: A REAPPRAISAL
Directed by GEORGE H. FORD, *University of Rochester*

   1. The 1890s: Genesis or Exodus
     HELMUT GERBER, *Purdue University*

   2. The Ivory Tower as Lighthouse
     RUTH ZABRISKIE TEMPLE, *Brooklyn College*

   3. George Moore and the 1890s
     GRAHAM HOUGH, *Christ's College, Cambridge University*

   4. The Early Yeats
     ALLEN R. GROSSMAN, *Brandeis University*

II. PROSE STYLE IN THE ENGLISH NOVEL
Directed by HAROLD C. MARTIN, *Harvard University*

   1. Prolegomena to the Analysis of Prose Style
     RICHARD M. OHMANN, *Harvard University*

2. The Prose Style of Tobias Smollett
   ALBRECHT STRAUSS, *Yale University*

3. Hardy and Burke's "Sublime"
   S. F. JOHNSON, *Columbia University*

4. Style and Anti-Style in *Vanity Fair*
   G. ARMOUR CRAIG, *Amherst College*

III. ATTRIBUTION BY INTERNAL EVIDENCE
   Directed by DAVID V. ERDMAN, *New York Public Library*

1. The Use and Abuse of Internal Evidence (examples from Smart
   and Johnson)
   ARTHUR SHERBO, *Michigan State University*

2. Two New Poems by Marvell?
   GEORGE DE F. LORD, *Yale University*

3. The Signature of Style (examples from Coleridge)
   DAVID V. ERDMAN, *New York Public Library*

IV. PATRISTIC EXEGESIS IN THE CRITICISM OF MEDIEVAL LITERATURE
   Directed by DOROTHY BETHURUM, *Connecticut College*

1. The Opposition
   E. TALBOT DONALDSON, *Yale University*

2. The Defense
   R. E. KASKE, *University of North Carolina*

3. Summation
   CHARLES J. DONAHUE, *Fordham University*

Registrants, 1958

Meyer Howard Abrams, Cornell University; Ruth M. Adams, University of Rochester; Gellert Spencer Alleman, Newark College of Arts and Sciences, Rutgers University; Mother Thomas Aquinas, O.S.U., College of New Rochelle.

Isabell Harriss Barr, Fordham University; Phyllis Bartlett, Queens College; Martin Carey Battestin, Wesleyan University; David W. Becker, Miami University; Dorothy Bethurum, Connecticut College; Siegmund A. E. Betz, Our Lady of Cincinnati College; Philip Bordinat, Miami University; Sister Mary Charlotte Borthwick, F.C.S.P., Providence Heights College; Hoyt Edwin Bowen, Pfeiffer College; Brother Clementian Francis Bowers, F.S.C., De La Salle College; the Reverend John Dominic Boyd, S.J., Bellarmine College; Sister Mary Brian, O.P., Rosary College; Mary Campbell Brill, West Virginia Wesleyan College; John Joseph Britton, S.J., Loyola University, Chicago; Cleanth Brooks, Yale University; Richard A. E. Brooks, Vassar College; Reuben A. Brower, Harvard University; Margaret M. Bryant, Brooklyn College; Mrs. W. Bryher, Vaud, Switzerland; Jean R. Buchert, Woman's College, University of North Carolina; Charles O. Burgess, College of William and Mary, Norfolk Division; Sister M. Vincentia Burns, O.P., Albertus Magnus College; Katherine Burton, Wheaton College.

Grace J. Calder, Hunter College; George Carr Camp, Southern Illinois University; Jackson Justice Campbell, Princeton University; Oscar James Campbell, Columbia University; John Stewart Carter,

Chicago Teachers College; Hugh C. G. Chase; John Aldrich Christie, Vassar College; the Reverend John Francis Coholan, Maryknoll Seminary; Robert A. Colby, Queens College; Zilpha Colee, Augustana College; William Bradley Coley, Wesleyan University; Ralph Waterbury Condee, Pennsylvania State University; John Allan Conley, John Carroll University; Frederick W. Conner, University of Florida; Francis A. Connolly, Fordham University; Allen Blow Cook, U.S. Naval Academy; Roberta Douglas Cornelius, Randolph-Macon Woman's College; William R. Coulter, Roanoke College; David Cowden, Swarthmore College; Alexander Cowie, Wesleyan University; George Armour Craig, Amherst College; William R. Crawford, Colby College; Licille Crighton, Gulf Park College; James H. Croushore, Mary Washington College; Charles R. Crow, University of Pittsburgh; James V. Cunningham, Brandeis University; John Vincent Curry, S.J., Le Moyne College; Sister Anne Cyril, S.N.D., Emmanuel College.

Charles Twitchell Davis, Princeton University; Richard Beale Davis, University of Tennessee; M. Elizabeth Dawson, Lindenwood College; Robert Adams Day, Queens College; Francis X. Degnen, St. John's University; Robert M. Dell, Pace College; Charlotte D'Evelyn, Mount Holyoke College; Sister Mary Aquinas Devlin, Rosary College; Sister M. Dolorita, St. Vincent Ferrer High School; Charles Donahue, Fordham University; E. Talbot Donaldson, Yale University; Sister Rose Bernard Donna, C.S.J., College of Saint Rose; David Joseph Dooley, Royal Military College of Canada; Georgia S. Dunbar, Hofstra College; C. Owen Duston, Wabash College.

Benjamin Weisiger Early, Mary Washington College of the University of Virginia; Edward R. Easton, Pace College; Ursula Elizabeth Eder, Brooklyn College; Merrie Einhorn, Columbia University; William Elton, University of California; George John Engelhardt, Loyola University, Chicago; David V. Erdman, New York Public Library; Sister Mary Estelle, O.P., Albertus Magnus College; Charles Kenneth Eves, City College, New York.

Arthur Francis Fenner, Jr., University of Notre Dame; Edward Fiess, New York State University College, Long Island; Edward

Garland Fletcher, University of Texas; Frank Cudworth Flint, Dartmouth College; Ephim G. Fogel, Cornell University; George H. Ford, University of Rochester; Sister Mary Francis, College of Mount Saint Vincent; Vincent Freimarck, Harpur College, State University of New York.

Harry Raphael Garvin, Bucknell University; Katherine Haynes Gatch, Hunter College; Helmut E. Gerber, Purdue University; Walker Gibson, New York University; Mary E. Griffin, Vassar College; Ray Ginger, Alfred A. Knopf, Inc.; Anthony Cabot Gosse, Brown University; Douglas Grant, University of Toronto; Helen Teresa Greany, Columbia University; Richard Hamilton Green, The Johns Hopkins University; Richard Leighton Greene, Wesleyan University; Mary Elizabeth Grenander, New York State University College for Teachers; Allen Richard Grossman, Brandeis University; Stanley S. Gutin, University of Pennsylvania.

John A. Hansen, Jr., University of Tennessee; Alfred B. Harbage, Harvard University; Mrs. Katherine Sumner Harris, Queens College; John A. Hart, Carnegie Institute of Technology; Allen T. Hazen, Columbia University; Eldon C. Hill, Miami University; William Bernard Hill, S.J.; C. Fenno Hoffman, Jr., Massachusetts Institute of Technology; Daniel G. Hoffman, Swarthmore College; John Hollander, Connecticut College; Vivian C. Hopkins, New York State College for Teachers, Albany; Lillian Herlands Hornstein, New York University; Graham Goulder Hough, Christ's College, Cambridge, England; Donald R. Howard, Ohio State University; Muriel J. Hughes, University of Vermont; Samuel L. Hynes, Swarthmore College; Julia H. Hysham, Skidmore College.

Sister Mary Immaculate, O.P.; Ruth M. Jackson, Simpson College; Lisle C. John, Hunter College; S. F. Johnson, Columbia University; Ruth E. Jones, University of Utah.

Robert E. Kaske, University of North Carolina; Ralph James Kaufman, University of Rochester; Norman Kelvin, University College, Rutgers University; John Pendy Kirby, Randolph-Macon Woman's

College; Henry W. Knepler, Illinois Institute of Technology; Stephen Kopman, University of Toronto.

James Craig La Drière, The Catholic University of America; the Reverend John P. Lahey, S.J., Fordham University; Seymour Lainoff, Yeshiva College; Gerard R. Lair, O.S.B., St. Mary's Abbey; the Reverend Henry St. C. Lavin, S.J., Loyola College, Baltimore; Lewis Leary, Columbia University; Ellen Douglass Leyburn, Agnes Scott College; Dwight Newton Lindley, Hamilton College; Jean S. Lindsay, Hunter College; Arthur Walton Litz, Princeton University; Laura Hibbard Loomis, Roger Sherman Loomis, Columbia University; George deForest Lord, Yale University.

Marion Kilpatrick Mabey, University of Connecticut; John Patrick McCall, Georgetown University; Charles J. McCann, Canisius College; John McChesney, Hotchkiss School; William Ulma McDonald, Jr., University of Toledo; John MacEachen, Fairleigh Dickinson University; Richard Macksey, The Johns Hopkins University; George McFadden, Temple University; Alan Dugald McKillop, The Rice Institute; Kenneth MacLean, Victoria College, University of Toronto; Vincent L. McMullen, St. John's University; Mother C. E. Maguire, Newton College of the Sacred Heart; Leonard F. Manheim, The City College, New York; Sister Elizabeth Marian, College of Mount Saint Vincent; Sister Julia Marie, College of Mount Saint Vincent; Mother Saint Rita Marie, Notre Dame College of Staten Island; Mary H. Marshall, Syracuse University; Harold C. Martin, Harvard University; Sister Joseph Mary, S.N.D., Emmanuel College; Louis Lohr Martz, Yale University; John Kelly Mathison, University of Wyoming; Harrison T. Meserole, Pennsylvania State University; Paul L. Millane, McGraw Hill Book Co., Inc.; Dorothy S. Milton, Ferris Institute; Francis E. Mineka, Cornell University; Louie M. Miner; Jean Misrahi, Fordham University; Sister Jeanne Pierre Mittnight, C.S.J., College of Saint Rose; Mother Grace Monahan, O.S.U., College of New Rochelle; Charles E. Mounts, University of Florida; Charles Murrah, University of Virginia; Andrew Breen Myers, Fordham University.

Sophia Phillips Nelson, West Virginia State College; Helaine Newstead, Hunter College; Elisabeth Ann Noel, Aquinas College; William Thomas Noon, S.J., Canisius College; Sister M. Norma, Albertus Magnus College; William R. North, Pennsylvania State Teachers College, Lock Haven; Gertrude Elizabeth Noyes, Connecticut College.

Robert M. O'Clair, Harvard University; W. H. Sterg O'Dell, Drexel Institute of Technology; Gerald Leo O'Grady, University of Wisconsin; Richard Malin Ohmann, Harvard University; Joseph Eugene O'Neill, S.J., Fordham University; James M. Osborn, Yale University; Charles A. Owen, Jr., University of Connecticut.

W. D. Paden, University of Kansas; Alex R. Page, University of Massachusetts; Stephen Curtiss Paine, Salem College; William J. Park, Columbia University; Alice Parker, Lindenwood College; John William Parker, Fayetteville State Teachers College; Sister Marie Paula, College of Mount Saint Vincent; Gretchen Paulus, Wellesley College; Robert O. Payne, University of Cincinnati; Norman Holmes Pearson, Yale University; Harry William Pedicord; Brooke Peirce, Goucher College; Marvin Banks Perry, Jr., Washington and Lee University; Abbie Findlay Potts, Rockford College; the Reverend Charles J. Quirk, S.J., Loyola University of the South.

Warren Ramsey, University of California, Berkeley; Isabel Elizabeth Rathborne, Hunter College; Charles Arthur Ray, North Carolina College at Durham; John Palmer Reesing, Jr., George Washington University; John K. Reeves, Skidmore College; the Reverend Terence Joseph Reynolds, Siena College; Warner G. Rice, University of Michigan; Louise E. Rorabacher, Purdue University; Mrs. Jonathan T. Rorer, Somers Historical Society; Rebecca Dorothy Ruggles, Brooklyn College; James D. Rust, Michigan State University.

C. Earle Sanborn, University of Western Ontario; James Lee Sanderson, Grove City College; Bernard Schilling, University of Rochester; Howard Hugh Schless, Columbia University; Helene B. M. Schnabel; Richard J. Schoeck, University of Notre Dame; Flora Rheta Schreiber, The New School for Social Research; Joseph Schwartz, Marquette University; Aurelia Grether Scott, Wagner College; Helen M. Scurr,

University of Bridgeport; Frank Eugene Seward, The Catholic University of America; Richard Sexton, Fordham University; Edgar Finley Shannon, Jr., University of Virginia; F. Parvin Sharpless, Jr., Drexel Institute of Technology; Arthur Sherbo, Michigan State University; Gordon Ross Smith, Pennsylvania State University; Nathan Comfort Starr, University of Florida; Ruth M. Stauffer, Hofstra College; John Keith Stewart, University of Cincinnati; Albrecht Benno Strauss, Yale University; Stanley Sultan, Smith College; Walter Eugene Swayze, United College, Winnipeg; the Reverend Paul Joel Sweeney, S.J., Xavier University.

Anne Robb Taylor, Connecticut College; Ruth Zabriskie Temple, Brooklyn College; Doris Stevens Thompson, Russell Sage College; Samson O. A. Ullmann, Union College; Howard P. Vincent, Illinois Institute of Techology; the Reverend Vianney F. Vormwald, O.F.M., Siena College; Richard Beckman Vowles, University of Florida.

Eugene M. Waith, Yale University; Andrew Jackson Walker, Georgia Institute of Technology; Regis P. Wallace, O.S.B., St. Mary's Abbey; Walter Weyler Waring, Kalamazoo College; Jeanne Welcher, St. John's University; Mother Elizabeth White, Newton College of the Sacred Heart; John W. Wieler, Hunter College; Edward Kneale Williams, DePauw University; Marilyn Lammert Williamson, North Carolina State College; William K. Wimsatt, Yale University; Calhoun Winton, University of Virginia; Matthew M. Wise, Roanoke College; Marion Witt, Hunter College; Samuel K. Workman, Illinois Institute of Technology; Philip S. Yedinsky, Drexel Institute of Technology.